WHAT IS THE MEAN

SAINSBURY CENTRE
Living Art Sharing Stories

Kulturalis

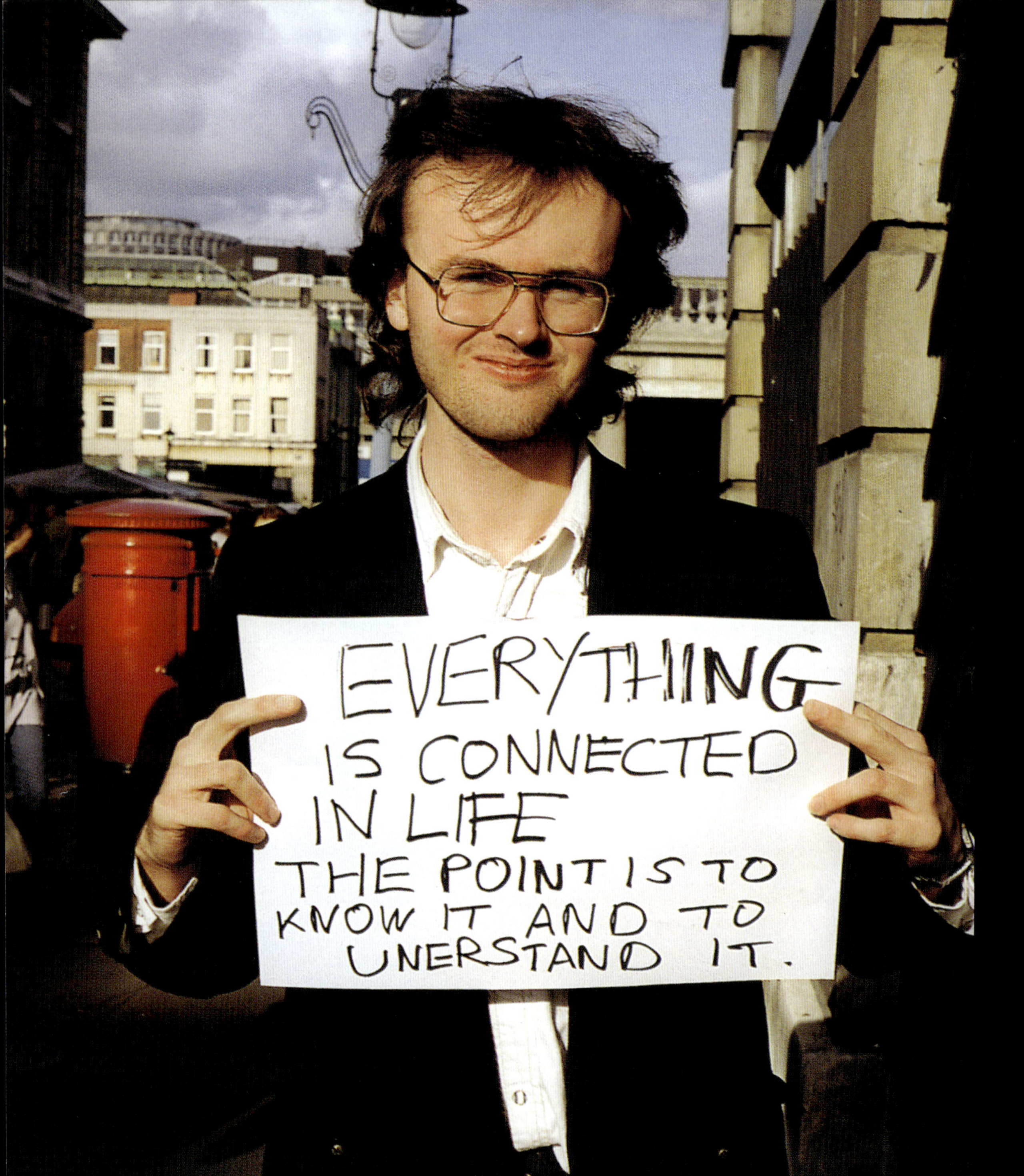
EVERYTHING
IS CONNECTED
IN LIFE
THE POINT IS TO
KNOW IT AND TO
UNERSTAND IT.

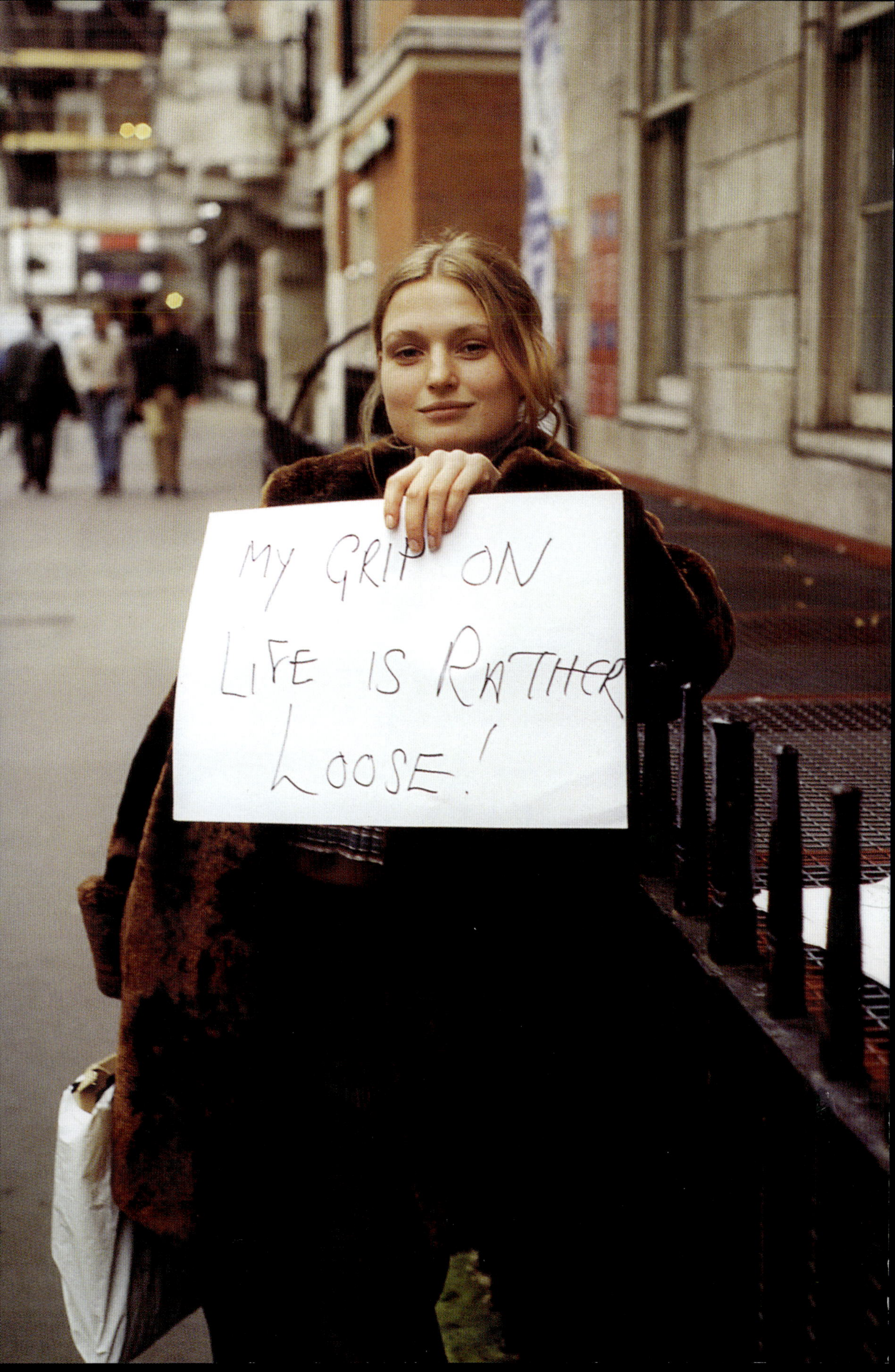
MY GRIP ON
LIFE IS RATHER
LOOSE!

Published to accompany the *What is the Meaning of Life?* season at the Sainsbury Centre, University of East Anglia, Norwich, Norfolk:

Living by the Rule: Contemporary meets Medieval
16 May – 4 October 2026

Play Power
16 May – 4 October 2026

Joy Like Time
20 June – 15 November 2026

New Commissions:
Life in the Multiverse: Libby Heaney

CATKINS FOREVER: Ruth Ewan

https://www.sainsburycentre.ac.uk

First published in 2026 by Kulturalis Ltd
14 Old Queen Street, London SW1H 9HP
United Kingdom
www.kulturalis.com

ISBN 978 1 83636 043 8

A catalogue record for this book is available from the British Library

Series Editor: Tania Moore
Project Manager: Lizzy Silverton
Design: James Alexander, Jade Design
Reproduction by Opero, Verona
Printed and bound in Czech Republic by PB Tisk, Příbram

EU GPSR Authorised Representative:
EASY ACCESS SYSTEM EUROPE OÜ, Mustamäe tee 50, 10621, TALLINN, Estonia
email: info@easproject.org

Front cover: Tacita Dean, *Paradise: Thrones* (detail), 2021, colour screenprint with a satin seal varnish on Somerset Satin Tub 410g
Page 2: Gillian Wearing, *Signs that Say What You Want Them To Say and Not Signs that Say What Someone Else Wants You To Say: EVERYTHING IS CONNECTED IN LIFE THE POINT IS TO KNOW IT AND TO UNERSTAND IT.*, 1992–3, c-type print on aluminium
Page 3: Gillian Wearing, *Signs that Say What You Want Them To Say and Not Signs that Say What Someone Else Wants You To Say: MY GRIP ON LIFE IS RATHER LOOSE!*, 1992–3, c-type print on aluminium

CONTENTS

FOREWORD
JAGO COOPER

Art is the raw, unflinching materialisation of human existence. So, when we search for the true meaning of life, what better guide can there be to help us than art? Art encompasses the universality of human experience, from across time and space, offering a tangible, real-world, empathetic and emotional connection that enables us to explore meaning from multiple perspectives.

You can trust an artwork. As you create or meditate upon a work of art, you can share your innermost thoughts, your unvarnished truths, because an artwork will always hold that confidence. Our role in life is so influenced, so controlled, by our relationships, by the people we share our lives with – from family and friends to bosses and employees. Yet, these relationships are often tightly framed within established social norms, the product of an accident of circumstance, as much as a carefully chosen plan.

This book uses art and material culture to shatter the illusion of established norms and to create alternative ways of seeing what the truth to life could be. The art examined in the pages that follow provides the imagination, motivation and inspiration required to find the meaning of life in the most unexpected of places.

Tacita Dean, *Paradise: Archangels, Principalities, Powers, Virtues, Dominations, Thrones, Cherubim, Seraphim*, 2021, colour screenprints with a satin seal varnish on Somerset Satin Tub 410g. Private collection

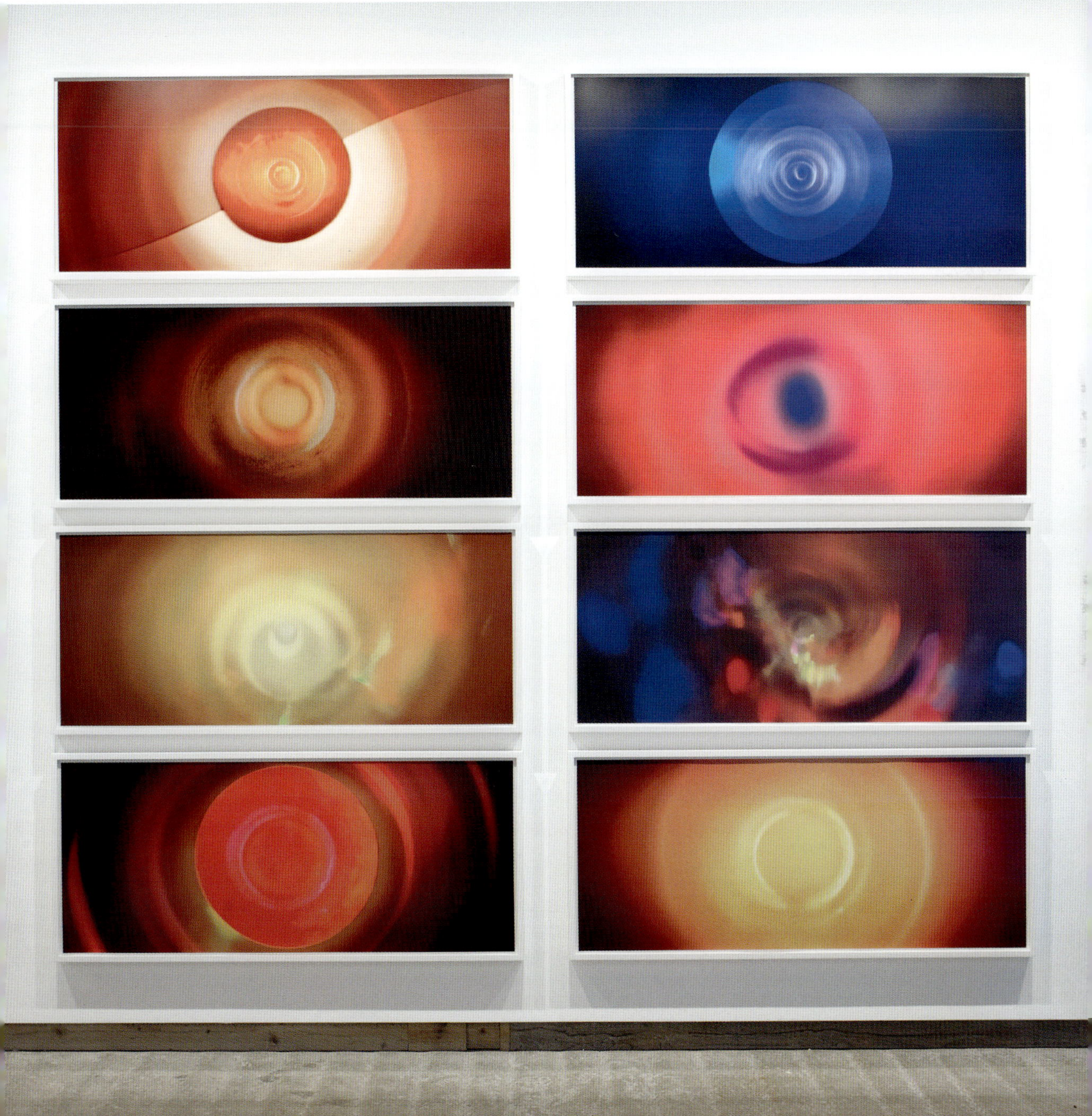

WHAT IS THE MEANING OF LIFE?

JAGO COOPER AND TANIA MOORE

Art answers the questions that we don't know how to ask. Here we explore how art can answer the question, 'What is the meaning of life?'

The arc of this book reflects the arc of life itself, beginning with childhood notions of playful exploration – of a world where life offers boundless opportunity – and ending with questions about what exists when life is taken away. Words often feel inadequate to take on such existential questions as the meaning of life, but as Leonora Carrington observed, 'There are things that are not sayable. That is why we have Art.'[1] Art materialises the indefinable essence of life. The artworks in this book provide the reader with alternative ways of framing the question, 'What is the meaning of life?', and offer them inspiration to find their own answers.

Ben Highmore's 'Glorious, Convulsive Frivolity: Wild Play' is the perfect introduction to that raw essence of what it means to be human. The word 'play' can often be used pejoratively, to belittle as inconsequential or childish. As Highmore so persuasively argues, play is often the most profound exploration of what it is to be human. Play is the mechanism by which we carry out the ultimate testing of boundaries, of realities and unrealities. We can use play to find out what the rules are, and to see which can be bent or even broken. Perhaps one of the many reasons play is so fun as a child is that we don't understand the relationship between rules and the consequences of breaking them. It is society that creates the rules by which we play, defining what is allowed, what is socially sanctioned. The work of documentary maker Humphrey Jennings (1907–1950), artist Eileen Agar (1899–1991) and others discussed in Highmore's chapter expose the fragility and fictional nature of such societal rules. The art of play punctures this illusion and calls into question how and why these rules are created in the first place.

As an adult, play often gets formulated into a world of well-organised games that are structured by socially agreed rules. The advantage of playing as an adult is that the building blocks of knowledge, and the stakes of the game, often grow and, as a result, become more profound. Samuele Tacconi takes on this examination of playing the game cross-culturally in his chapter, 'Deities, Mighty Queens and Heroes at Play: Games in Human Societies'.

Tacconi's research teases out how the study of the rules of games in different cultures reflects divergent societal values and meanings of a good life. His work draws on a material world spanning thousands of years, from the Maya ball courts of tropical Central America to the invention of chess in South Asia. These games become a mechanism of social interaction to foster, test and forge the culturally specific values of human relationships. Games can be a safe space for social interactions, politics and even open warfare. Tacconi's discussion of 'playing the game' as a proxy for 'living in the real world' is eloquently made. It exposes the ability of the human species to invest so much truth, emotion and raw humanity into the meaning and consequences of an abstract action. The outcome of a ball passing through a hoop, or one piece of wood

Shirley Baker, *Young girls playing in the street – Hulme, Manchester*, 1965, photograph

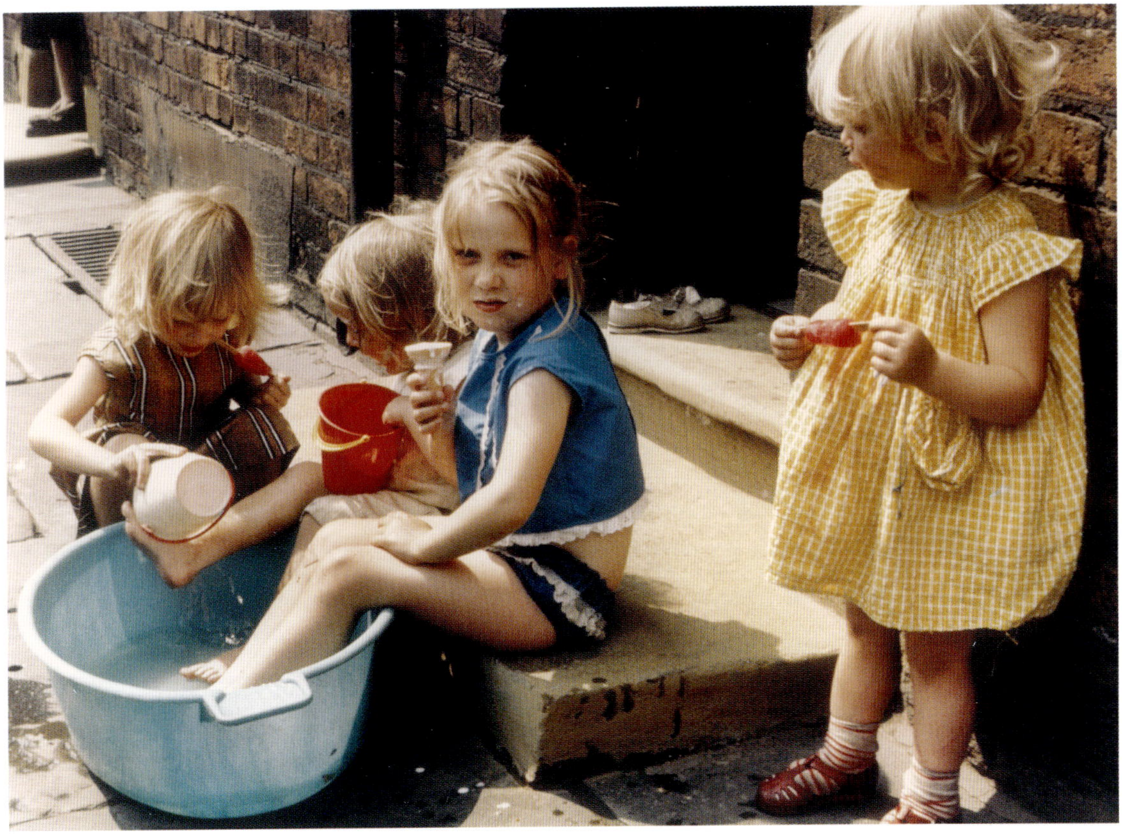

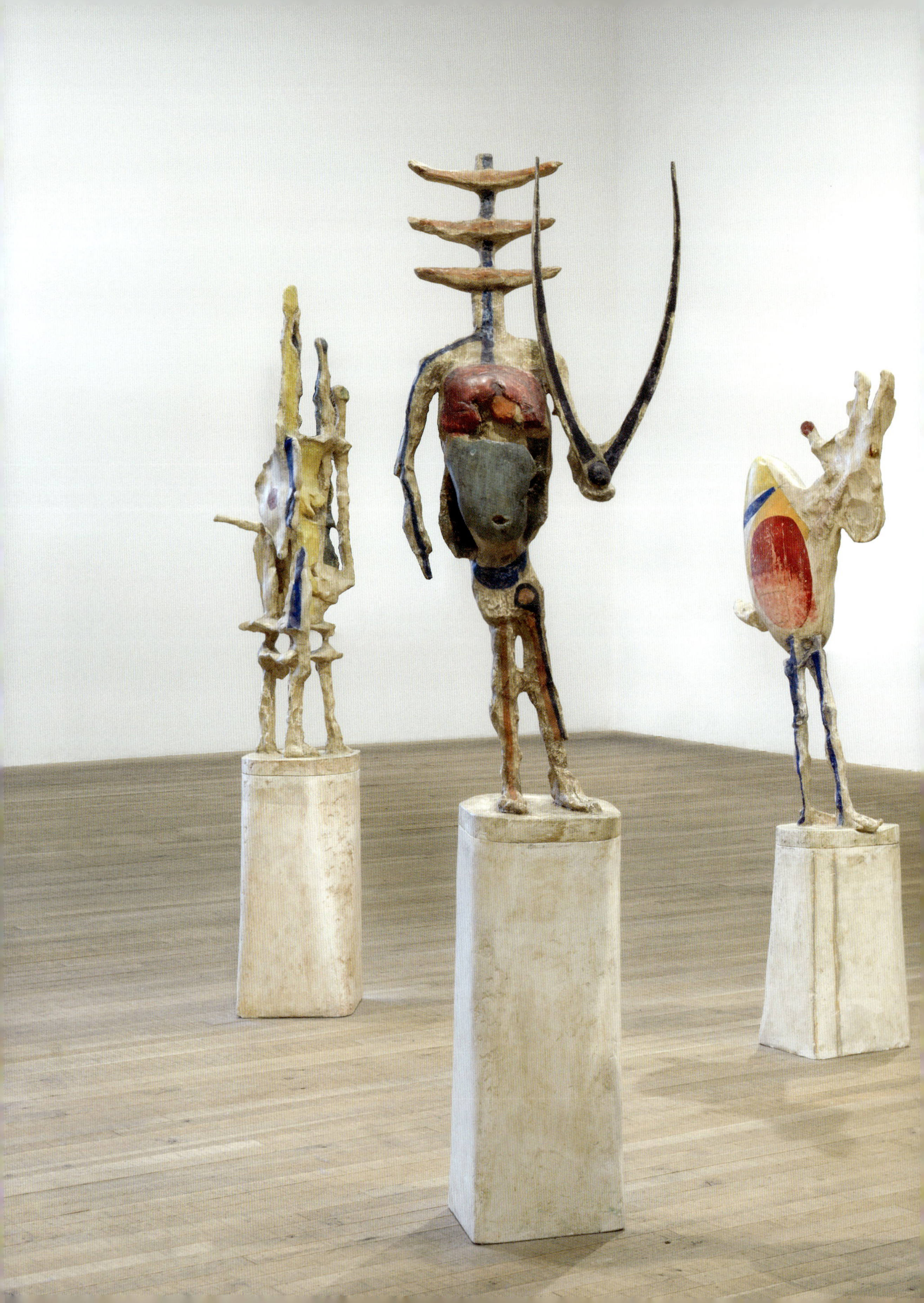

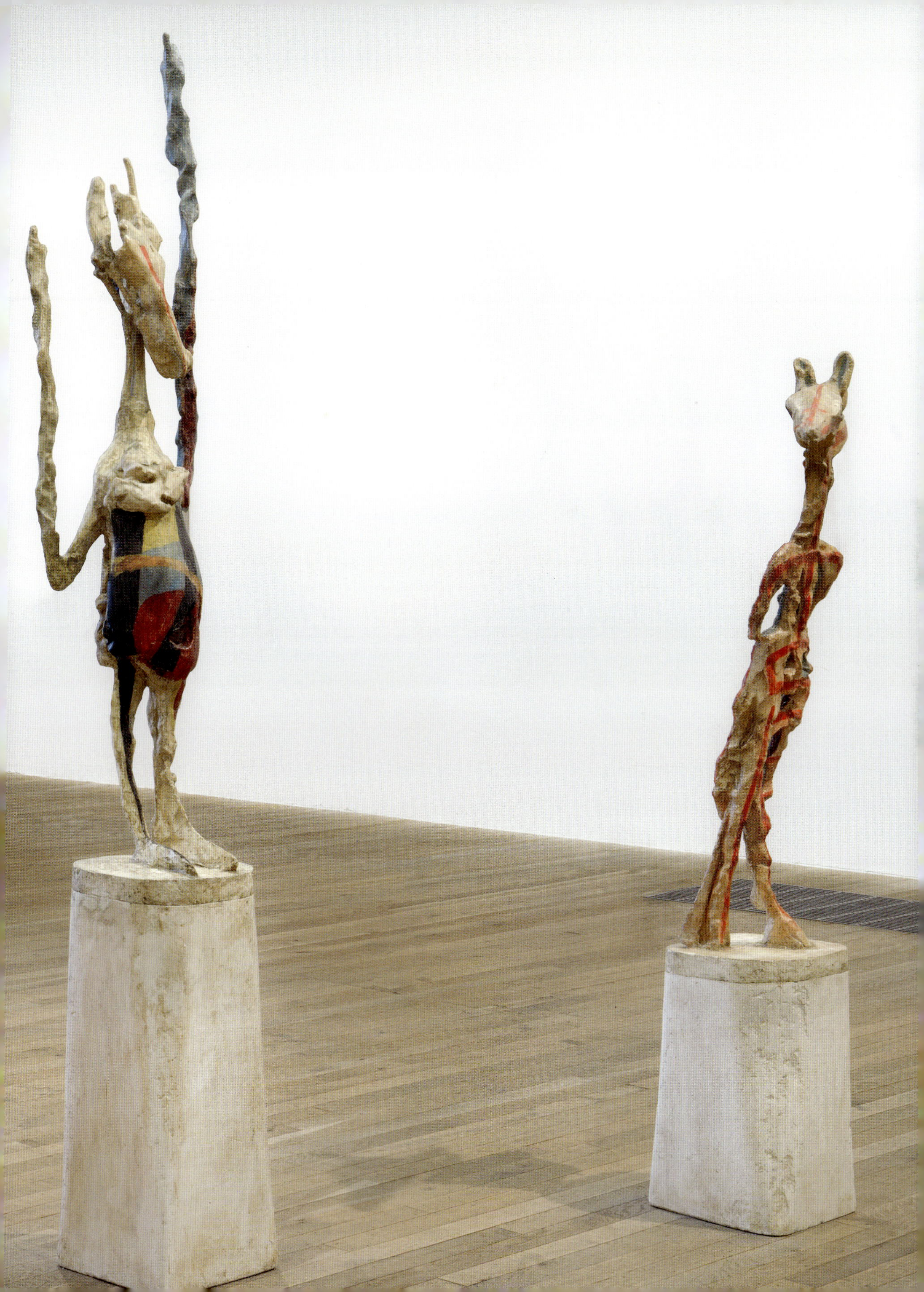

[previous page] Germaine Richier, *Chessboard, Large Version*, 1959, painted plaster. Tate

on a board 'taking' another, become genuinely life changing in the real world. The game of chess has been inspirational for artists, from Honoré Daumier (1808–1879) in the 1860s, to Marcel Duchamp (1887–1968) and Germaine Richier (1902–1959) in the twentieth century. Yoko Ono (b.1933) created a simple but significant shift when she made the typically black-and-white board purely white in *Play it by Trust* (1966). The single colour relied on players' trust and memory, ultimately rendering the game impossible and reflecting the artist's pacifist political views.

Using the material world to create fantasy, or 'parallel' worlds, enables us to live out all possible alternatives. The similarities between enacted ancient scenarios for other existences and contemporary discussions of multiverse worlds connects this human fascination with the consequences of choice across the ages. It reflects how age-old tools for human questioning of the decisions we take, and the pathways we might forge in our lives, are always used, no matter what state of technological development we may live within. This ability for emotional projection, and the real-life jeopardy of a game, results in an extraordinary shift. It raises questions of belief and faith, as the games we play become a metaphor for life. Tacconi draws out this higher thought, exploring how different societies see themselves as the pawns of a greater game played by the gods.

If 'Wild Play' captures the contemporary world of play, and 'Games in Human Societies' the historic rules by which different cultures play them, then 'Living by the Rule' is a trans-historical connection between the two. This chapter carefully considers the interplay between human constant and cultural context, between lived reality and political landscape. As Jessica Barker and Ed Krčma reveal, art is, and always has been, one of the most pervasive and powerful tools to communicate the rules of life. The altruism of the crucifixion, the serenity of the Virgin Mary and the omnipotence of the ruling monarch have long communicated the rules of power. The art and architecture of churches and cathedrals demonstrate how to worship God, as well as indicating the values by which the congregation should live their lives. The social norms and established political hierarchy can be told to the people without the clumsy need for the written or spoken word.

One of the many advantages of art in this role is that it isn't bound by the rigidity with which written laws and decrees often are. The experience of art is contingent on physical context and individual experience. In exploring and extrapolating this point in the unwritten rules of medieval and contemporary art, Barker and Krčma play out the nuance of human desire for understanding, and the powerful attraction that concepts of simplicity and clarity can have for people, particularly in a world that can often feel so far beyond the control of the individual. In offering up simple rules by which a 'good life' can be controlled and achieved, art can create a trans-historical constant of the human desire to have meaning in life and an ability to achieve it.

The clarity of this argument is exposed so well in their critique of modernism, as a counterpoint to medievalism, in which the artistic desire to break the rules exposes the untethered nature of society. Does the modernist uncoupling of individual actions from social norms provide more meaning to life, or expand beyond the horizon the directions in which meaning might be found? This dialectic disruption and expansion of possibilities in modernism as a counternarrative to the simplicity and conformity of the Benedictine *Rule* exposes the challenges of the modern world. A modern world in which the role of art can be subverted. It is resonant that the twentieth-century commercialisation of art has been 'corrupted' by the capitalist frameworks of a globalised world, in which market forces drive a new set of social rules. It is apt that these new rules are so clearly embodied in the changing landscape for the art world – a market worth $50 billion, communicating the ascent of a new world order. Such societal transformation is laid bare by the beautiful juxtaposition of medieval and contemporary art worlds and societal rules.

This use of time as a comparative analytical tool for establishing meaning and understanding societal transformation is poetically picked up in 'Joy Like Time' by John Kenneth Paranada. Paranada reveals how time is often the construct by which meaning is controlled. The exploration of time as a framework of societal control reveals how a better understanding of its role can inform how it is thought of by individuals. Artists have broken time; broken these schedules of norms to expose other temporalities. *The Artist Is Present* (2010) by Marina Abramović (b.1946) (illustrated on p. 53) uses time at a human scale to refocus the truth that it is human relationships that formulate meaning. For this performance, Abramović spent three months in the gallery space, and the audience were invited to sit in an empty chair opposite her. Over 1,500 people connected silently with the artist across 700 hours.

The power of Paranada's treatise is that anyone can activate art as a mechanism to challenge time and temporality in life. In exposing how artworks themselves exist in a different time and temporalities than human lifetimes, it enables the contact point between individual and artwork to be outside the rules of time. This temporal disruption and interplay between the individual and the societal are exposed in *Signs that Say What You Want Them To Say and Not Signs that Say What Someone Else Wants You To Say* (1992–3) by Gillian Wearing (b.1963), as the real questions of life and meaning are laid bare.

The exceptional insight of the artistic and curatorial lens in this chapter is that meaning in life is a 'verb not a noun', that action and dynamism are what formulate meaning, not the passive and static abstracted thoughts about what meaning could be. The ability of such an idea to inspire action and purpose is in itself the inspiration to find the meaning of life. By thinking deeply about your own existence, and how this is impacted by the different temporalities of your lived experience, it exposes

Susan Morris, *SunDial: Nightwatch_Sunshine_2012* (detail), 2024, jacquard tapestry with cotton and linen yarn

how art can provide a temporal fluidity and dynamism within which to think about life.

From the multitemporal to the multiversal, in her chapter 'Life in the Multiverse', Rosy Gray examines the work of artist Libby Heaney. Heaney's output takes the pursuit of the meaning of life literally into another dimension. Her work draws on her exceptional experience as a quantum physicist to hypothesise the fragility of the 'real' in the world around us. Heaney's art imagines responses to the unimaginable riddles that science creates but can't answer. Echoing the untethering of the modernist critique by Barker and Krčma, this work is as awe-inspiring as it is disconcerting. To question the meaning of life is also to question what exists without it; such a starkness forces the ultimate distillation of thought and beliefs. Heaney's work *Life in the Multiverse* (2025) immerses us in a world of sliding doors and alternative realities. It exposes us to reflections on what our lives are like in worlds where we have taken different decisions, where the road forks and the pathway back may be blocked in this world but already exists in another. She provides the privilege of imagining those different lives before returning to our own. This world of split realities, only moving forwards along the narrow ridge of one's own timeline, materialises the sense of jeopardy we all feel. Have we made the right decisions? Heaney's work inspires us to think about this because, after all, if we are going to travel along such a precarious path, it seems wise to take a little time to think about the desired destination.

There is no doubt that art provides the inspiration required to consider the journey of life. Each of the authors and artists in this book provide a different piece of equipment to employ along the way, from play, to games, to rules, to timelines, to alternative realities. These are the tools that expose the questions required to arrive successfully at the end.

GLORIOUS, CONVULSIVE FRIVOLITY: WILD PLAY

BEN HIGHMORE

Two boys are hurtling down what looks to be an improvised runway. The photographer, Henry Grant (1907–2004), has caught them both in mid-air, momentarily disconnected from their shadows. Others in the background look poised to follow them. From their clothes we can see that it's the 1970s, and the image caption tells us that this is an adventure playground in the London Borough of Hackney. It is an image crammed with social history (a history of experimental playgrounds and of successful post-war multiculturalism in Britain), but there is also something that transcends history, and indeed geography. Give a bunch of kids a dramatic slope and someone is bound to run down it, slightly out of control, in the grip of a gleeful desire to hurtle forward, unbound. If this is play, and I know that it is, then what can we say about it? What does it mean, and what does it feel like? The exuberant fun that characterises aspects of play at its most delicious and hilarious, but also its most fleeting and evanescent, is hard to marshal into a world of meaning.

This doesn't mean that such marshalling hasn't been attempted. You don't have to look very far to see how central play is to invention, creativity, learning, development, and on and on. Ask me the question of how play exists as a meaningful aspect of life and I could find you a dozen experts – from psychoanalysts to physicians – who would explain how significant play is for children in processing change, especially traumatic change; how important it is for developing gross and fine motor skills; and how crucial playful mimesis (play-acting versions of the adult world) is for socialisation. It wouldn't be hard to find others who would champion the play-based world of games and sports, particularly team sports, on the grounds that they teach an ethos of team spirit and camaraderie as well as instantaneous decision-making and strategic planning. But, still, where does this leave my chaotic, spontaneous, joyful, perhaps even 'stupid' fun of hurtling down a steep slope?

That effervescent fun of careening along a zip wire seems to belong most intimately to a specific period of childhood. The zenith of our attraction to (and ability to enjoy) this sort of mindless fun appears to be between eight and 12 years old: a time before the self-consciousness of puberty and adolescence has got its fangs into our souls. The guileless and impulsive enjoyment of the body and the erasure of the ego seem to be especially easy at this time of life. But we can see lots of echoes of it as we age: slapstick and gross-out comedy; wild dancing (rave culture, for instance); various means of intoxication; sexual abandonment; forms of musical improvisations (free jazz, trance); and so on. Perhaps in a darker hue, and for those attracted to aggression, it can be seen, in a distorted form, in the violence of town centres on a Friday night. This may be youthful rough-and-tumble played out, often with more serious consequences, in adult bodies. Full-tilt running down a hill, and its ilk, are forms of play that we should distinguish from a more docile world of games and 'pretend' playing – perhaps we should call it 'wild play'.

Henry Grant, *Playground, Hackney Marshes*, 1978, photograph. Museum of London

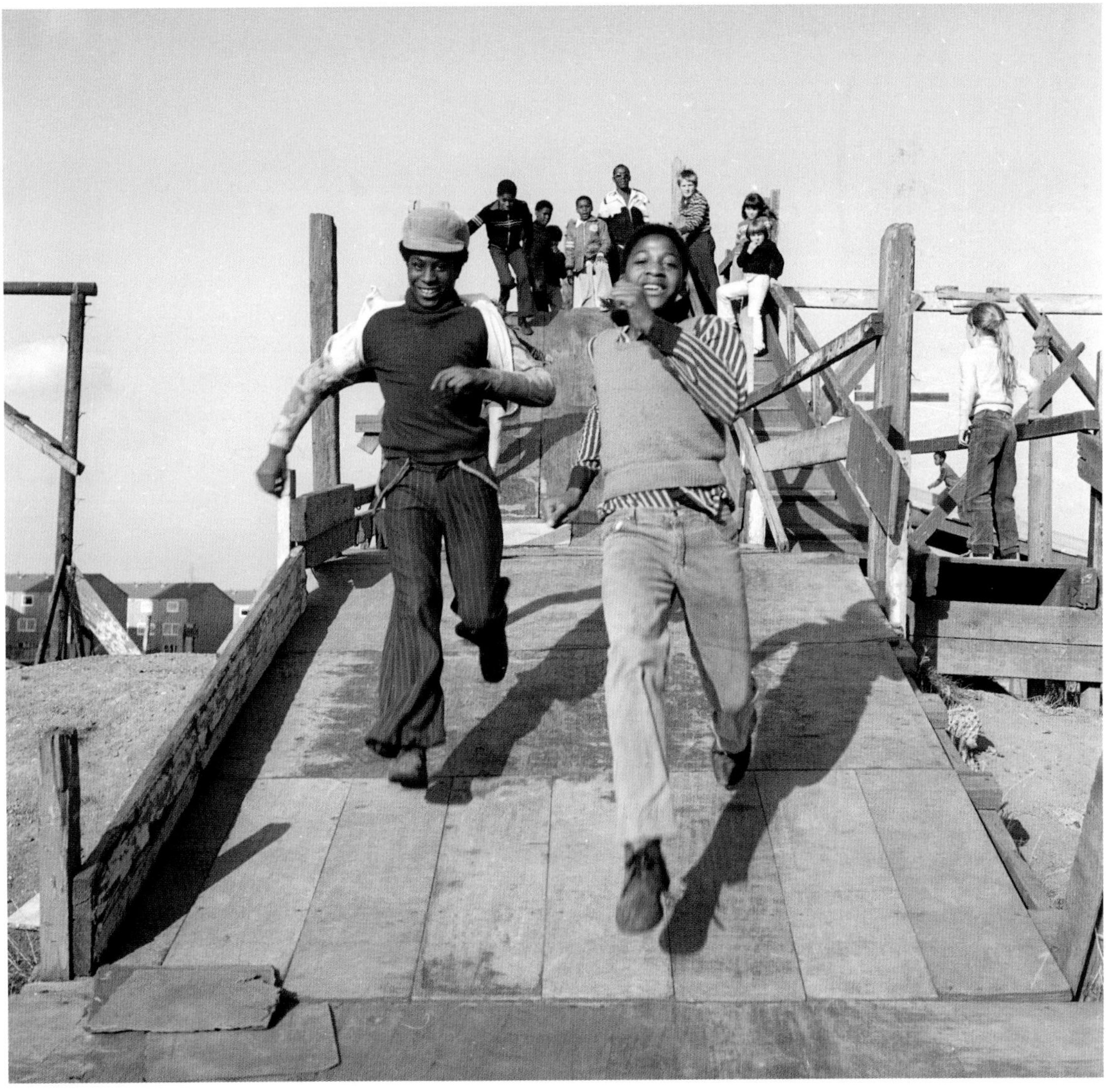

Roger Mayne, *Adventure playground, Islington [boy on zip wire]*, August 1963, photograph. V&A

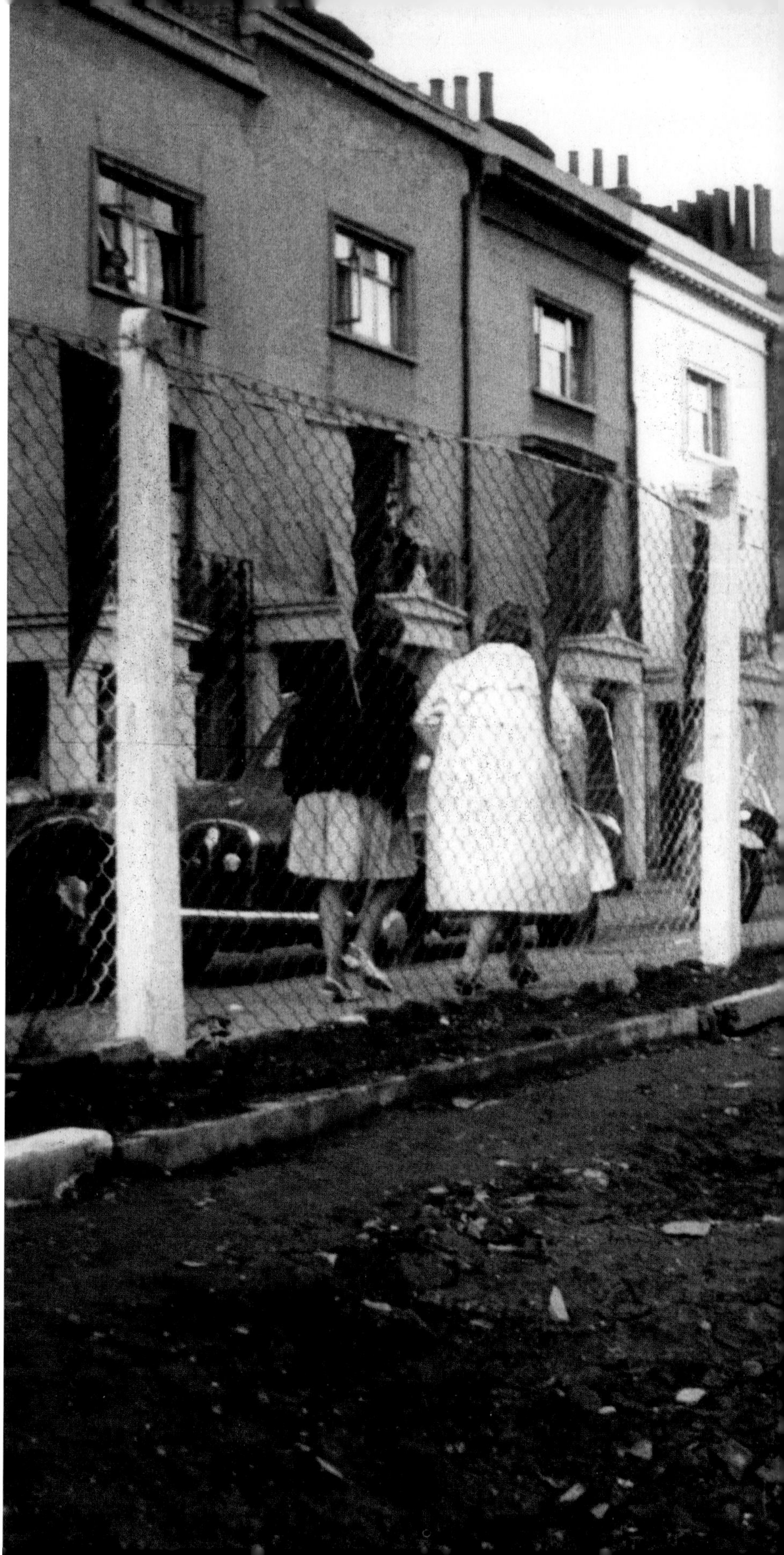

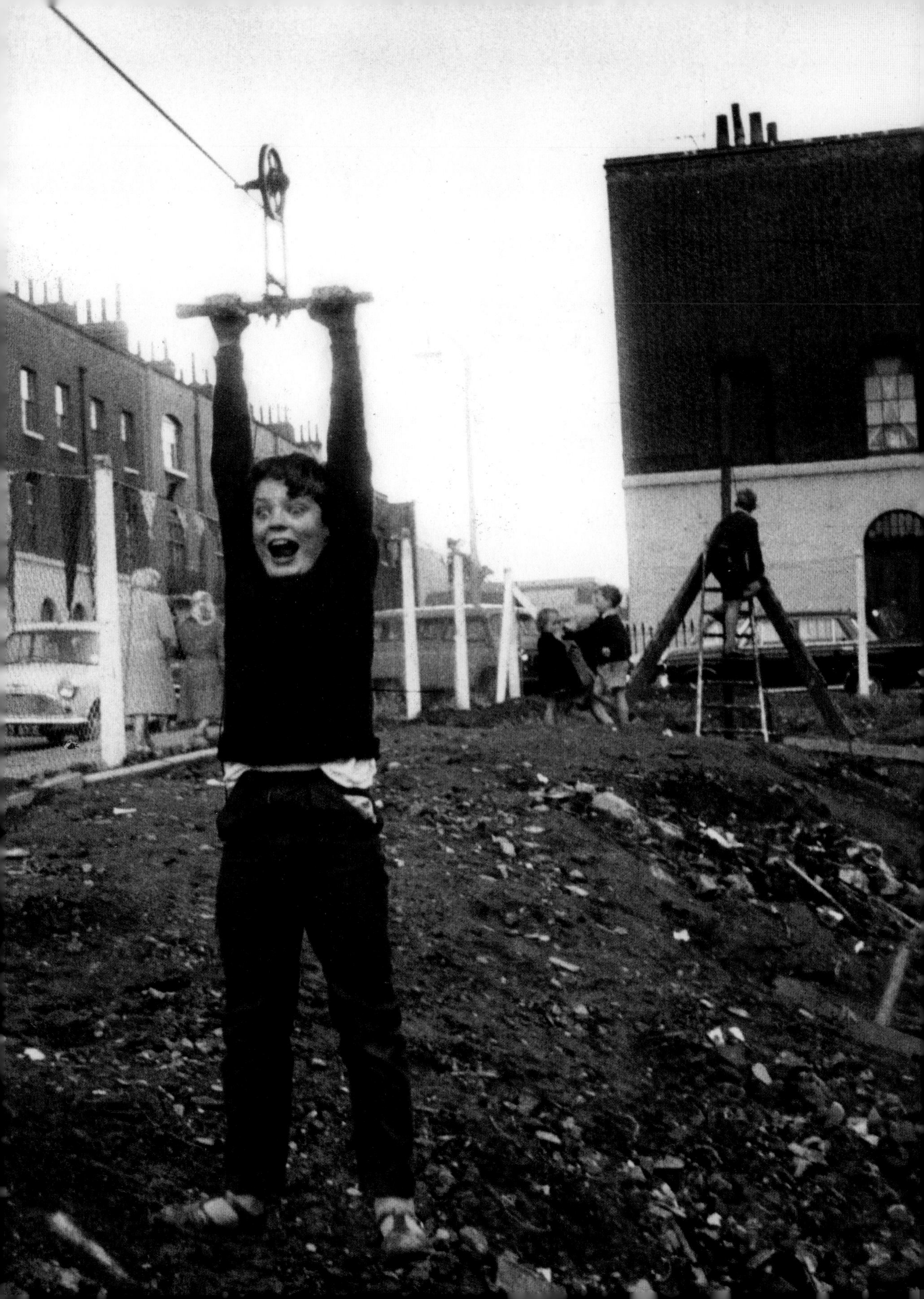

L. S. Lowry, *Lancashire Fair, Good Friday, Daisy Nook,* 1946, oil on canvas. Government Art Collection

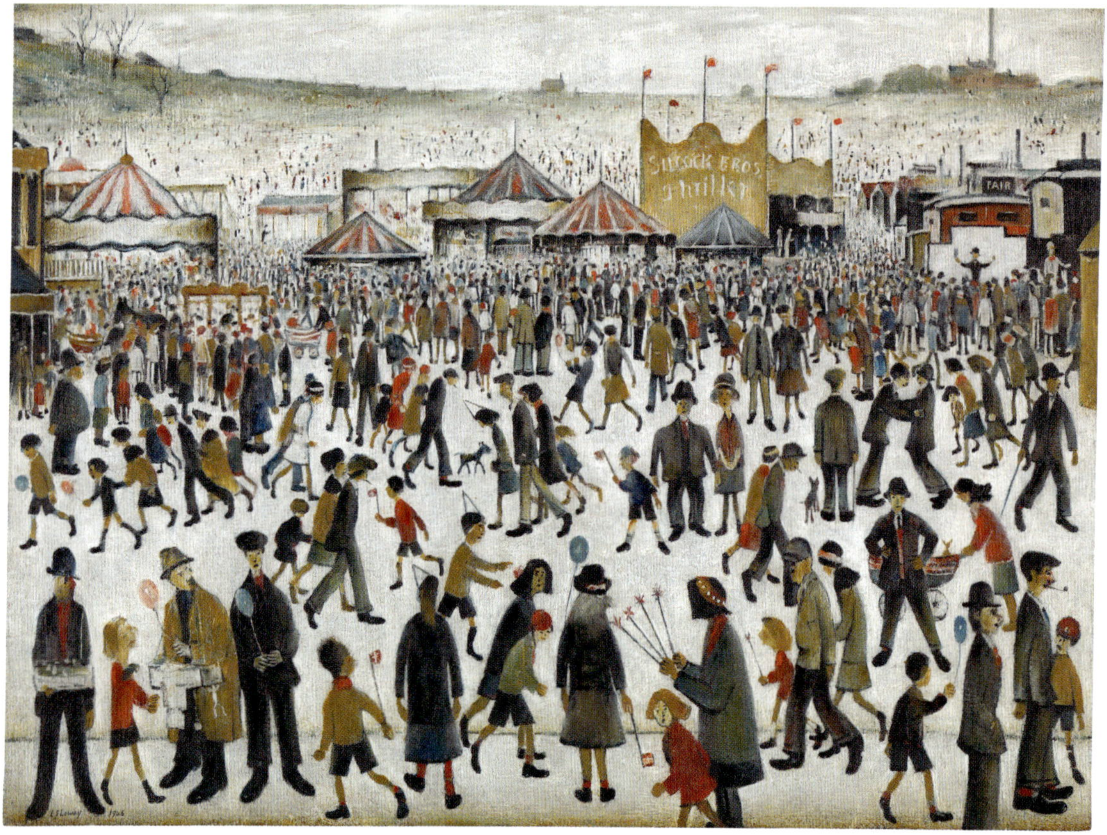

Eileen Agar, *Ladybird*, 1936, gelatin silver print with gouache and ink. The Murray Family Collection (UK & USA)

odder version of surrealism, that met under what now feels like the deeply ironic title of the Collège de Sociologie.[6] This was a group that included Georges Bataille (1897–1962), Roger Caillois (1913–1978) and Michel Leiris (1901–1990), among others. What distinguished this version of surrealism was that it sensed that wild play was already fully alive in the world, if only you knew where to look. Theirs was a more anthropological version of surrealism that was attentive to the non-rational, not as a strategy for making disruptive art, but as a guiding force that could be found across the globe in all sorts of rituals and various milieux. In their studies of the ancient world, of non-Western culture and of secret societies within the West, wild play wasn't the rare ingredient of a disciplined society, but was instead the flame that humankind worked to keep alive.

The world of wild play cannot simply be captured as a social good, nor can we easily recruit it as central to the *meaning* of life. It isn't that sort of phenomenon. It is resistant to being corralled into an ideational world. We need to think about it differently. We could consider it as a life force, an energy, a cultural physics; something that we would sorely miss were it to be entirely absent from our lives. What would it mean for society if this kind of energy was suppressed completely? A world that fears risk and danger in play (though not in corporate and planetary strategy) and concentrates solely on growth and productivity? What would happen to these involuntary and convulsive pleasures if there were no outlets for them? Perhaps it is time to take them, if not seriously (which would be deeply contradictory), then at least on their own terms. To visibly treasure the frivolities of the everyday and to encourage new forms of wild play. Repress them and who knows what sort of grim and morbid derivations and deviations of wild play will emerge. Faced with the question, 'What is the meaning of life?', one answer would have to be 'wild play', but only if we understand 'meaning' as something like 'force' or 'vital energy'.

DEITIES, MIGHTY QUEENS AND HEROES AT PLAY: GAMES IN HUMAN SOCIETIES

SAMUELE TACCONI

Play is as serious as it is fun. When children play, their enjoyment is so all-encompassing that nothing is more important to them. They conjure up entire worlds as a setting for their playful narratives, requiring an absolute commitment to their own imagination. This aspect of childish play is not entirely lost in adulthood. What are rituals and myths if not an adult at play? Cosmic realms are reimagined in myths and acted out in performances, where players must operate by given rules and impersonate certain characters. Over time, these ritual performances have become more than the sum of their parts, transforming into societal structures and even religious practices.[1]

Malleable and playful myths – recounting tales of deities, monsters and heroes – have accompanied human history for millennia. They have been the primary way by which people have sought meaning, calling upon them to answer the great mysteries of existence and to offer solace against the ineluctability of death.

In human history and across cultures, ritual festivals, such as carnivals, have allowed people to play in order to communicate with the gods and to explore the human condition and the divine unknown, within the merriment of a festive occasion. The Greek philosopher Plato cited forms of play as constituting a good life. He wrote:

> One should live out one's days playing at certain games – sacrificing, singing and dancing – with the result that one can make the gods propitious to one-self and can defend oneself against enemies and be victorious over them in battle.[2]

Even when play among children or animals looks violent, it is typically governed by rules that separate it from actual fighting. Indeed, play is often regulated by more or less explicit rules that circumscribe its scope. Social norms can often resemble game rules. For instance, the religious commandments in pre-modern societies could sometimes feel more like the rules of a game that everyone had to play by than the dictates of a righteous god. In ancient Mesopotamia, an Akkadian text listing 'sins', known as *shurpu*, included such dictates as the prohibition of pointing at a lamp or asking for something in bad weather. They do not emanate from rational morality; rather, they are the rules of a game of cosmic proportions, where some players can impersonate gods and play as kings, while others will have to content themselves with smaller roles. This may sound like 'Dungeons & Dragons', but it is the starting point of a civil society.

Many rituals are, at their core, forms of play. Take for instance the *Ch'a Cháak* ceremonies held by Mayan communities in Yaxuna, Mexico, to summon rain. As part of the ritual, the best hunter is sent into the night to hide, while others must search for and retrieve him. This is a crucial part of the ritual. For Catholic participants in Yaxuna, this is a very serious business. Yet, to an outsider, it will resemble an elaborate version of hide-and-seek.[3]

Play is fun, but it can also be deadly serious. When two chess grandmasters face off at a

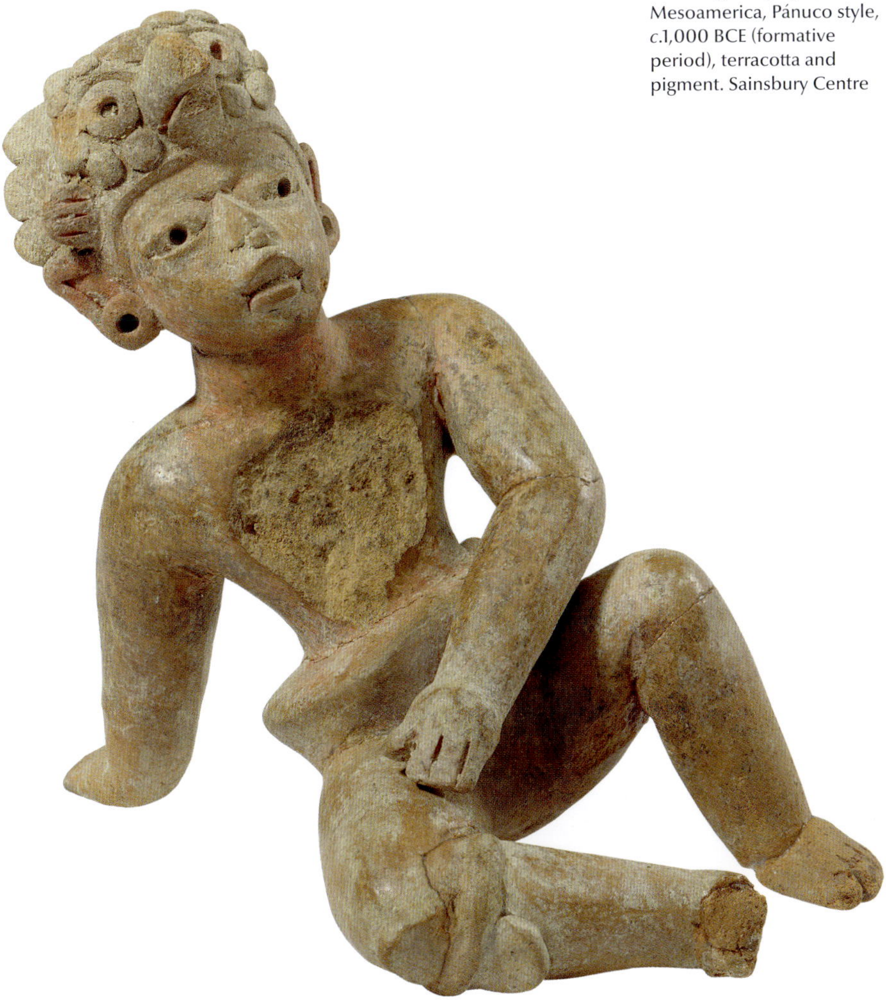

Reclining ball player, Mesoamerica, Pánuco style, *c.*1,000 BCE (formative period), terracotta and pigment. Sainsbury Centre

tournament, their intense focus leaves no room for frivolity. In ancient Mesoamerica, the stakes were even higher. Ball-game players sometimes risked their lives in matches that were simultaneously sports competitions and ceremonies. A miniature figurine from the Sainsbury Centre's collection, dating to the middle of the first millennium BCE, shows a reclining player in the act of striking the ball with his/her waist – a dynamic pose celebrating the physical prowess of the players and a testament to the long-standing relevance of this game to Mesoamerican cultures.

Ball courts in Maya and Aztec cities were not simply playgrounds; they were also sacred and political arenas, and not just for humans. According to Maya mythology, the gods themselves were ball players. In the *Popol Vuh*, the K'iche' Maya sacred text, the ball game plays a central role in a cosmic narrative about the creation of the world, where heroic humans and underworld gods clash in an epic contest. Violent as it may have been, the Mesoamerican ball game often acted in real life as a controlled substitute for open warfare.

Sports and games have often served in human societies as a form of ritually circumscribed conflict. First Nations people of the Great Lakes region developed a version of lacrosse that functioned as an alternative to war. These games channelled

Royal statue (*ndop*), Kuba-Bushong, Democratic Republic of Congo, seventeenth or eighteenth century, camwood. British Museum

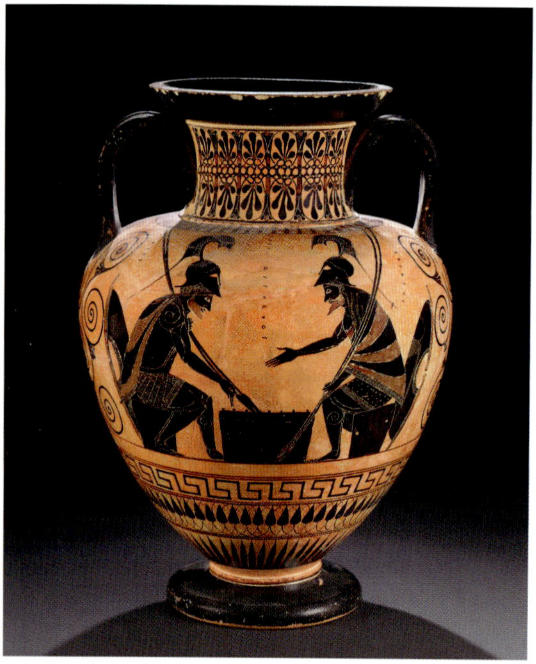

Attributed to Lysippides Painter, Amphora, *c.*530 BCE (Archaic Greece), ceramic. British Museum

tension and rivalry into structured competition, providing a safety valve for social pressures. Ritual competitions have often served as mechanisms of social stability in many cultures. In Polynesia, a physical competition known as *tangata manu* (bird man) was held on Rapa Nui (Easter Island) annually until the nineteenth century. It involved a swimming and climbing race to collect the first sooty tern egg on a nearby islet. Competitors included the representatives of different clans, who would participate on behalf of their leaders to gain the right to govern the following year.[4]

Duels and competitive games abound in Homer's *Iliad*, where aristocratic heroes engage in competitions with one another, performing roles as exemplars of heroic virtue. Epic duels, such as those between Achilles and Hector, followed formalised protocols of honour, closely resembling the athletic competitions of Ancient Greece. The connection ran both ways, as athletes in Panhellenic sports events re-enacted these epic duels, tracing their lineage back to the warrior-heroes of the Homeric poems. In Ancient Greece, victorious athletes were regarded as semi-divine beings, capable of channelling the gods' favour towards their community.[5]

In a well-known scene depicted on several Athenian black-figure amphorae, Achilles and Ajax are shown playing a board game – possibly *pessoi*, thought to resemble modern draughts or backgammon. They are fully armed, poised for battle, and yet off-guard and totally absorbed in a game, sometimes with the chaos of war raging in

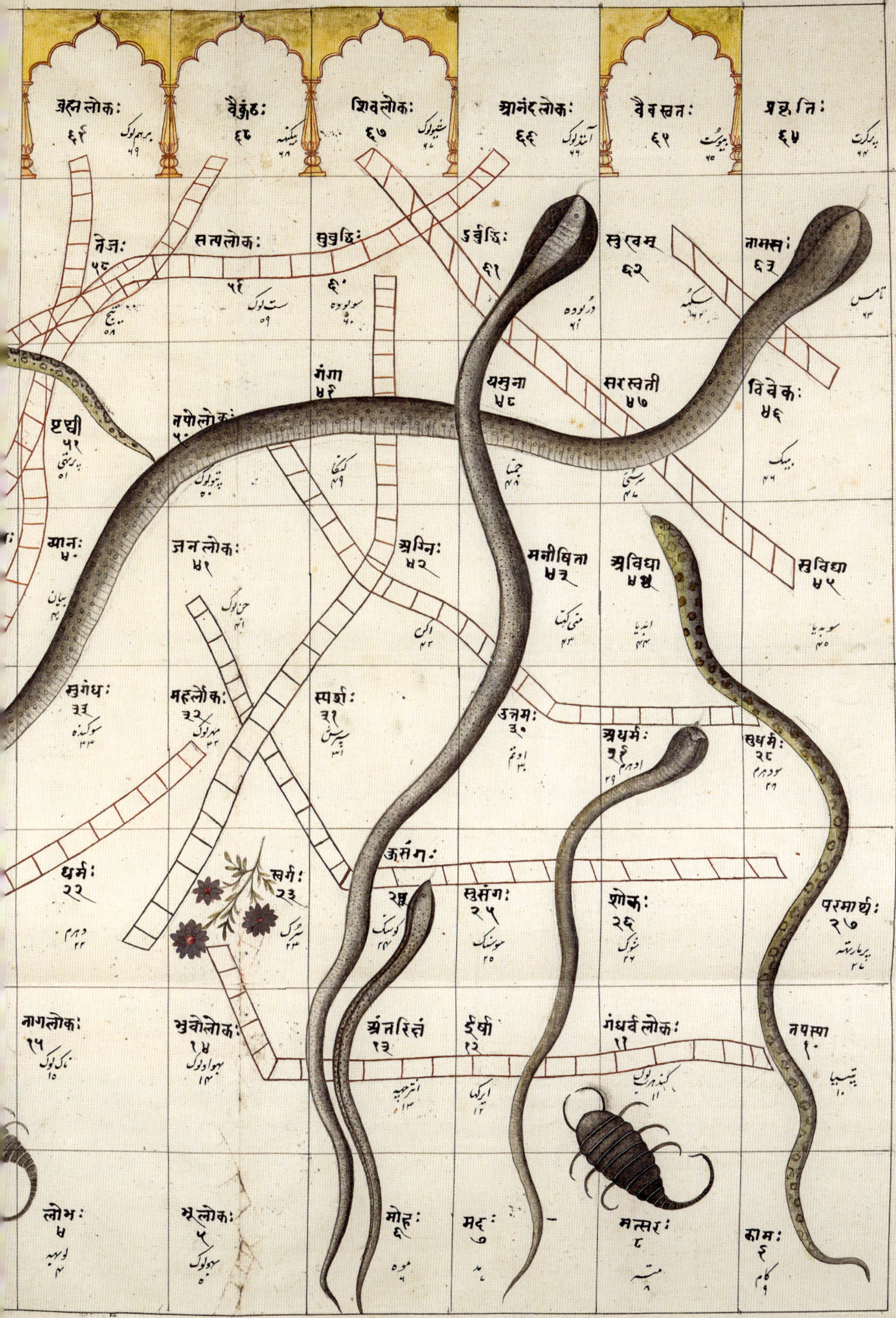

ब्रह्मलोक: ६९
वैकुंठ: ६८
शिवलोक: ६७
आनंदलोक: ६६
६५
प्रकृति: ६४
तेज: ५८
सत्यलोक: ५९
सुबुद्धि: ६०
दुर्बुद्धि: ६१
६२
तामस: ६३
पृथ्वी ५१
तपोलोक: ५०
गंगा ४९
यमुना ४८
सरस्वती ४७
विवेक: ४६
मान: ४०
जनलोक: ४१
अग्नि: ४२
४३
अविद्या ४४
सुविद्या ४५
सुगंध: ३३
महर्लोक: ३२
स्पर्श: ३१
उत्तम: ३०
अधर्म: २९
सुधर्म: २८
धर्म: २२
स्वर्ग: २३
कुसंग:
२४
सुसंग: २५
शोक: २६
परमार्थ: २७
नागलोक: १५
भुवर्लोक: १४
अंतरिक्ष: १३
ईर्षा १२
गंधर्वलोक: ११
तपस्या १०
लोभ: ४
भूलोक: ५
मोह: ६
मद: ७
मत्सर: ८
काम: ९

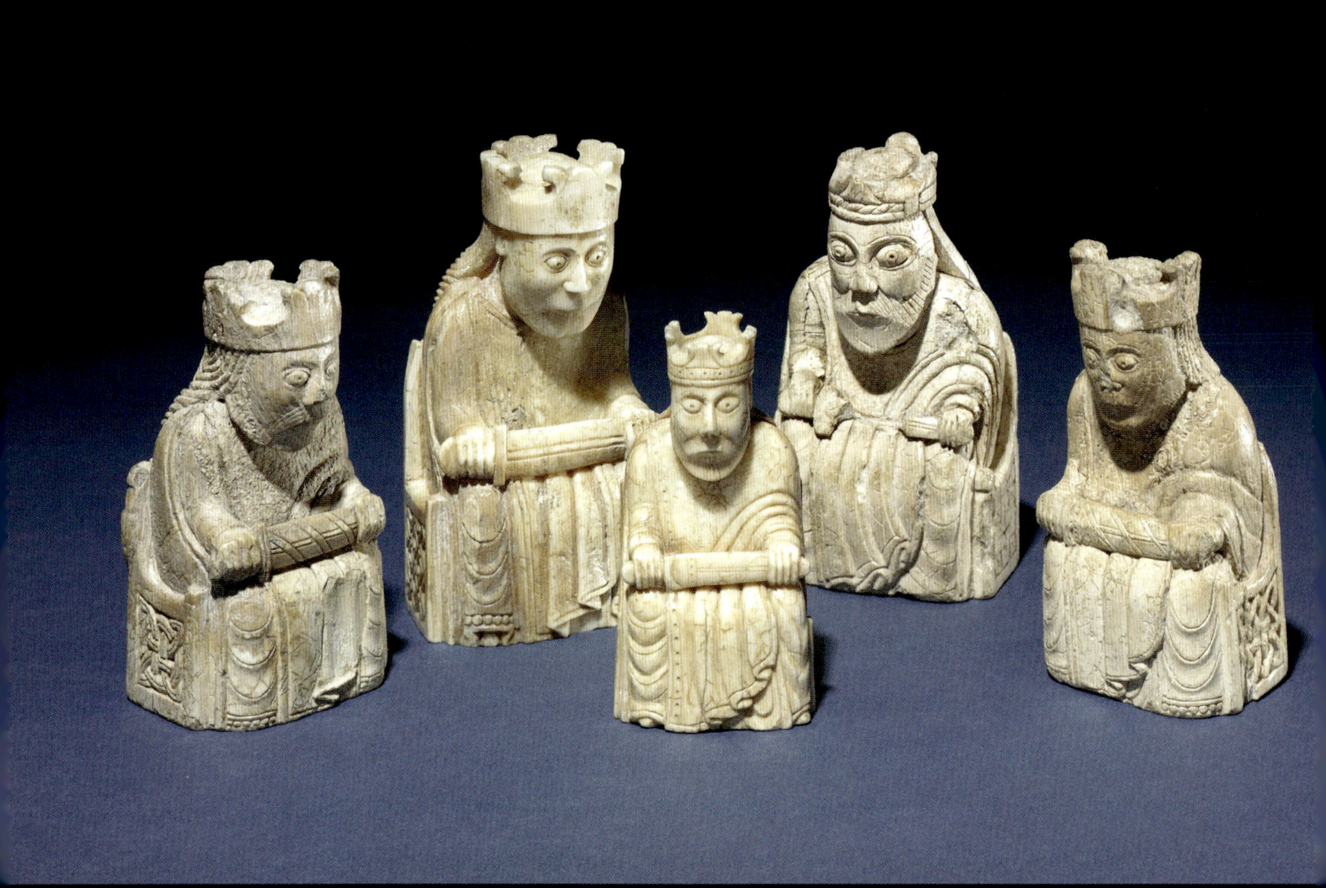

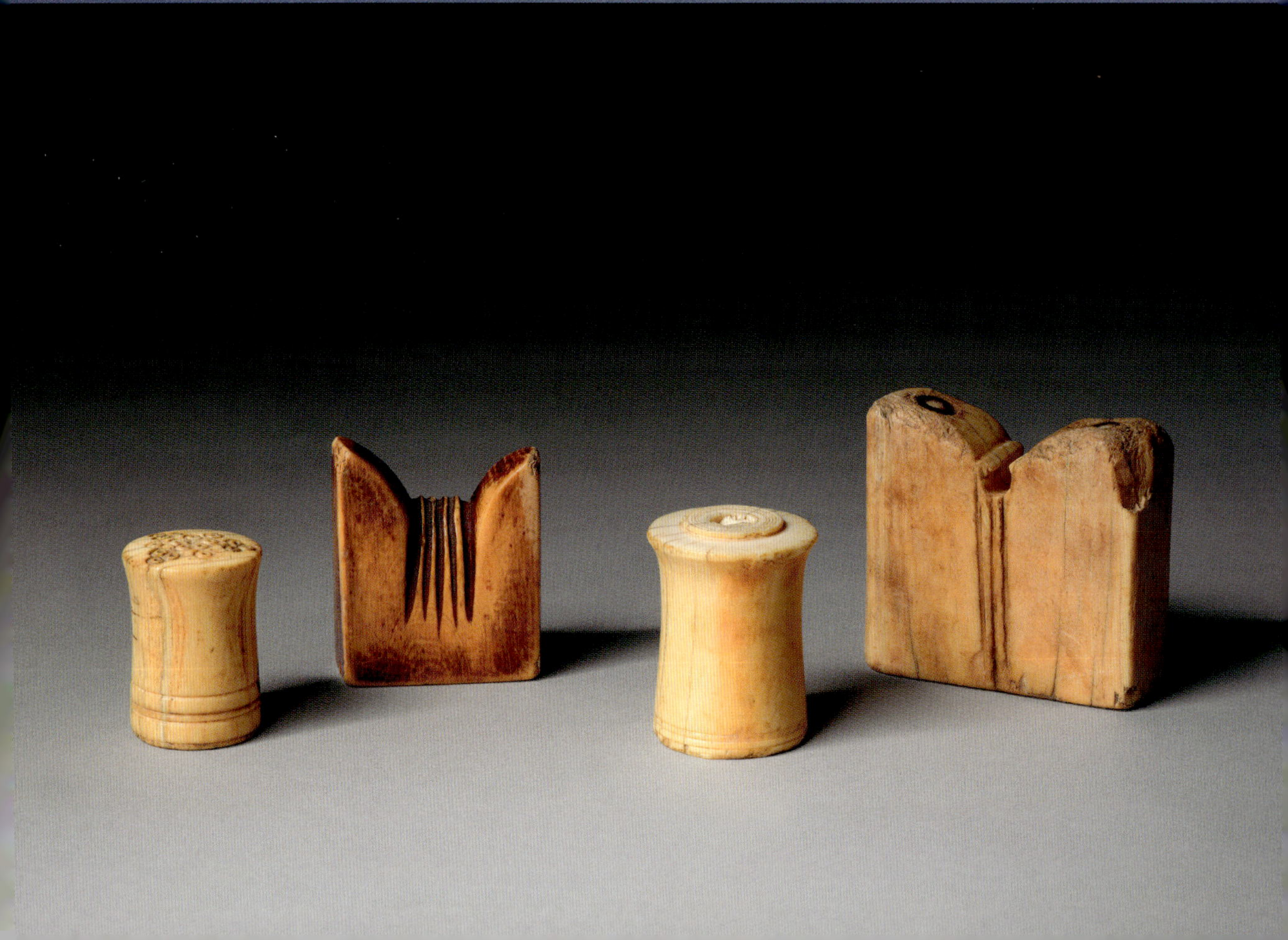

The Lewis Chessmen, probably Norway, *c.*1150–75, walrus ivory. British Museum

Gaming pieces from a chess set, probably Egypt, seventh–eighth century, ivory. Ashmolean Museum

Chance, indeed, is a crucial element of many games. The casting of lots or dice has an irresistible allure for humans. They offer a controlled way to flirt with the unknown. The thrill of gambling lies in its ability to mimic fate: we predict outcomes under uncertainty, risking something of value for the possibility of reward. This makes it not only entertaining but also deeply meaningful.

Unsurprisingly, the same tools used in gambling – dice, lots and other tokens – also became instruments of divination: a decision-making technology used by many cultures. Randomness has been seen by humans as a message from a divine or ancestral source. To cast lots was to open a channel to the will of the gods or spirits. In the Bible, the apostles cast lots to determine who should replace Judas Iscariot, trusting that the outcome would reflect their late leader's will (Acts 1:23–26). Perhaps, it is not entirely by chance that the word 'clergy' is etymologically linked to the Greek *kleros*, meaning 'lot' or 'chance'.

The overlap between gambling and divination has deep historical roots. Ancient Roman emperors were known to gamble with much enthusiasm, while in Indigenous North America, gambling was just as widespread – though often with very different social effects. According to archaeologist Warren DeBoer, women in some First Nations communities played high-stakes dice games with women from neighbouring villages, wagering shells and other valuables.[10] These games were not simply about entertainment; they often functioned as mechanisms for redistributing wealth across communities. The items used as stakes travelled vast distances by being continuously wagered – won, lost and won again – passed from hand to hand through networks of play.

Games, like rituals, are rarely neutral. They are often gendered – both in terms of who is allowed to play and of the symbolic roles assigned within the game. But these roles are not fixed. The evolution of chess pieces offers a vivid example of how cultural meanings shift over time. In medieval Islamic chess sets, the pieces were typically abstract and aniconic, reflecting religious norms. When the game spread to Europe, its imagery changed as well. The elephants of the original Indian game (*chaturanga*) turned into bishops, as shown by the highly celebrated, elegantly carved Lewis chess pieces, made in ivory. The king's vizier transformed into a queen – eventually becoming the most powerful piece on the board. This change reflected not only European cultural values but also the growing visibility and political clout of powerful queens in early modern Europe.[11]

Chess, like many games, became a metaphor for life itself. As Plato used *pessoi* to model the life of a good citizen, others have used chess to represent the rules and roles of society. Kings, queens, bishops and pawns all had their place on the board, and all had their limits. Even divine rulers had to move according to the rules of the game.

Eventually, this metaphorical use of games turned literal. In nineteenth-century Prussia, the gamification of reality became a military technique. Military planners developed a game called

Kriegsspiel ('war game'), loosely based on chess but adapted to simulate real battlefield scenarios. Over time, it was developed into a sophisticated training tool, complete with detailed topographical maps and rule sets that mimicked the complexities of actual warfare. The Prussian, and later German army gained a competitive advantage owing to the use of this game-based system of strategic education. *Kriegsspiel* proved so effective that it was still being used by German officers during the Second World War – even though Adolf Hitler himself disliked games and frowned upon the military use of *Kriegsspiel*. (If nothing else, this speaks volumes in favour of games.)[12]

Games can be bent to serve many different purposes. The symbolism of each playing space on a game board has often been used to create narratives of protests or satire – reflecting on the traits, tensions and absurdities of a given society. A game board can become a microcosm of a social landscape, exploring themes as diverse as the perils of capitalist monopolies, or the moral lessons of vice and virtue, displayed as snakes and ladders. Through these imagined journeys, games offer us a mirror – sometimes playful, sometimes biting – of the worlds we live in.

Play is a quintessential aspect of humanity. As humans, we play for many reasons: we play for life and death; for money and success; for knowledge and control; for divining or changing our fate. Heroic humans play, and so do sinister gods. Just as children engrossed in the act of play cannot fathom anything more important than it, so too as adults we get lost in our own games. Play remains central to even the most serious endeavours; we play at life, and, in turn, play makes life worth living.

C. H. Parnall, *The Western Approaches Tactical Unit*, 18 March 1945, photograph. Imperial War Museums

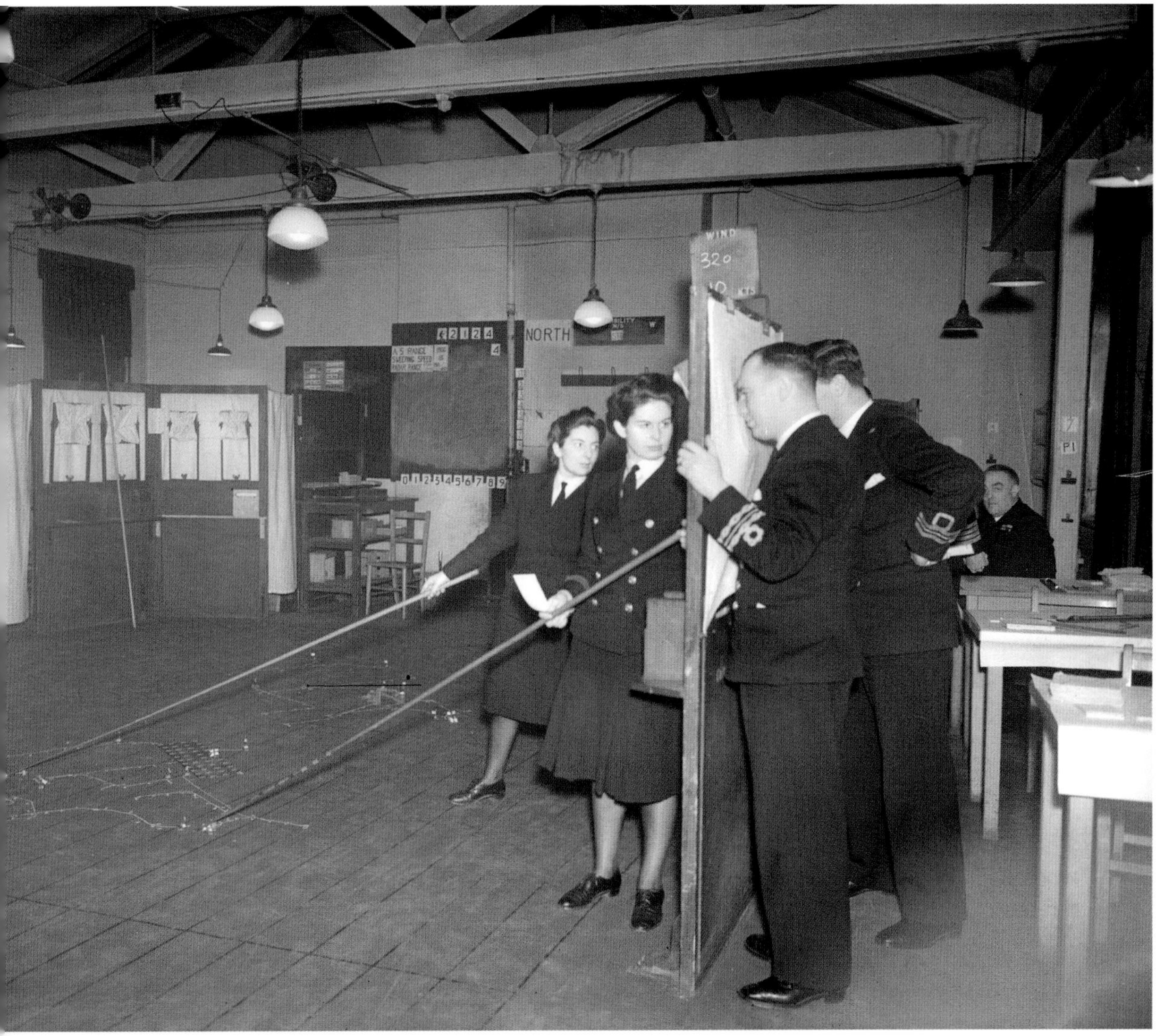

LIVING BY THE RULE
JESSICA BARKER AND ED KRČMA

Benedict enthroned, from the *Eadui Psalter*, Christ Church, Canterbury, *c.*1012–23, ink, pigments and gold leaf on parchment. British Library

Just as we began writing this text, news was announced of the withdrawal of NHS funding from our local hospice – 'efficiency savings'. This decision will mean depriving the community of a place that offers the possibility of a death closer to what one might choose. It is a small story amongst many larger ones, but one that says a great deal about the rule by which our contemporary lives (and deaths) are organised: while we cannot risk upsetting the bond markets, and while private banks are deemed too important to be allowed to fail, the possibility of a dignified death – let alone of a fulfilled life – is laid to waste. If a human being were merely a collection of molecules, such concerns would not be at issue. Indeed, the very fact of the impossible question that the Sainsbury Centre extravagantly poses – 'What is the meaning of life?' – intervenes in a gap (produced by inertia? Exhaustion? Negligence? Silencing?) and brings this situation into focus: we are that kind of being for which meaning is a problem.

The *Rule* of St Benedict

While the question of life's ultimate purpose has long been unanchored from shared certainties, the routines of daily existence continue to constitute a space from which meaning might nevertheless emerge. Our exhibition, *Living by the Rule: Contemporary Meets Medieval*, presented as part of the *What is the Meaning of Life?* season, explores this by focusing on the idea of rules and rule cultures: the interwoven fabric models, patterns, laws

William Howarde 1592

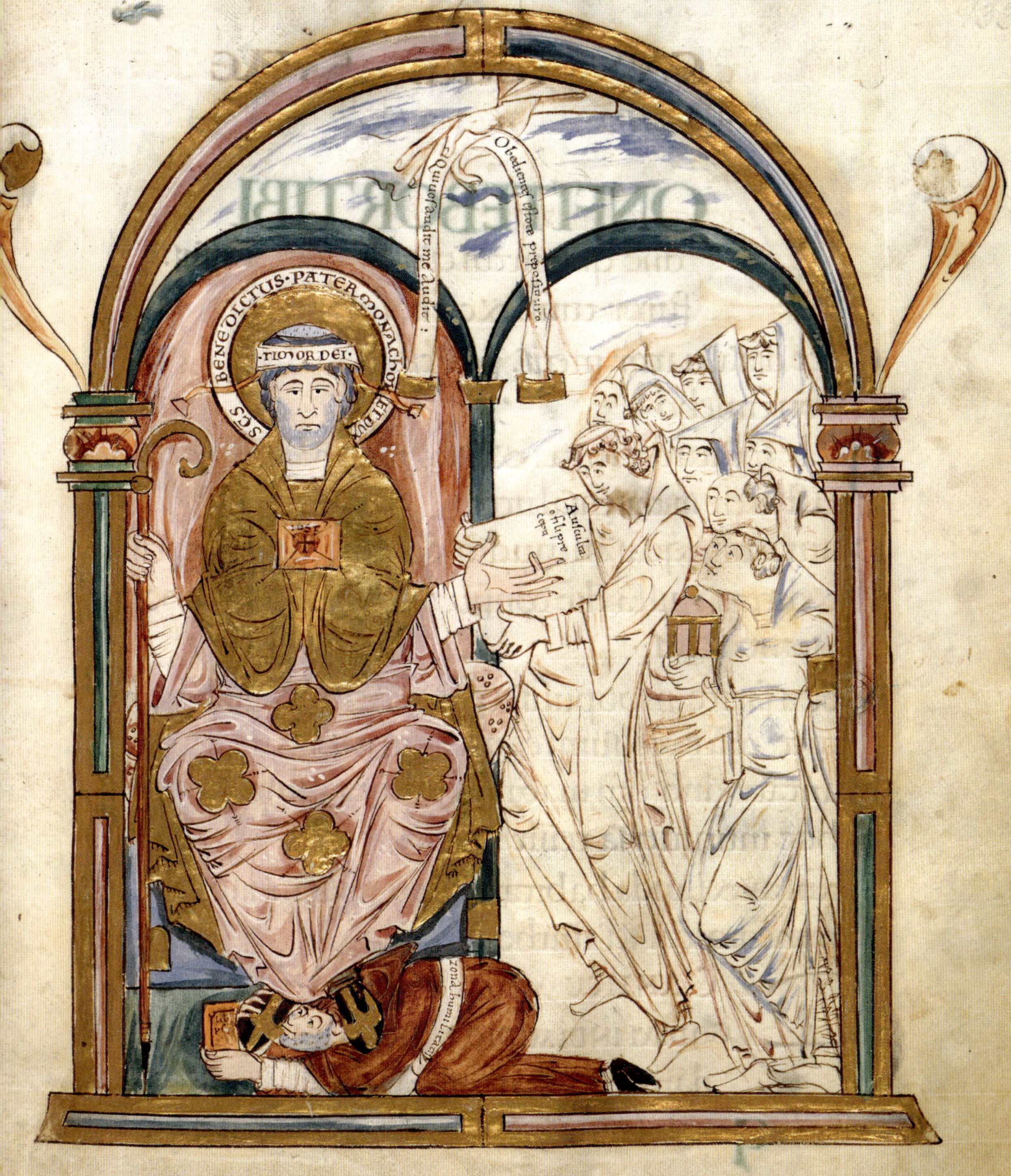

Angel with a harp,
East Anglia, *c.*1420, oak.
Wyvern Collection, London

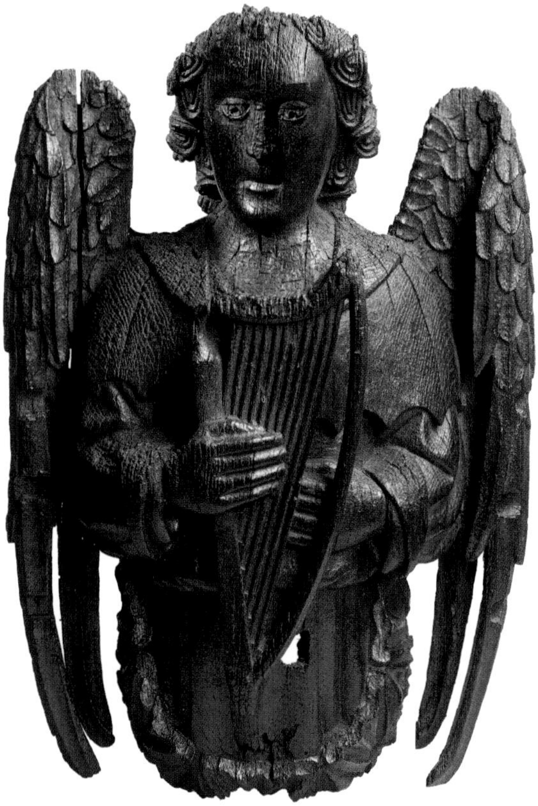

and regulations that structure daily life. It does this by placing contemporary conditions in dialogue with a strong, seemingly alien counter-image: that of medieval monasticism. And within monasticism – itself a diverse, trans-historical, global phenomenon – we focus on the *Rule of St Benedict*, written *c.*535–45 by the Italian monk, Benedict of Nursia (480–547), during a time of great political and social turbulence.

Benedict founded a monastic community at Monte Cassino, a mountainous wilderness in southern Italy. His *Rule* offered a framework for a radically different kind of life. He conceived it modestly as a 'toolkit' for the establishment and maintenance of a self-sufficient community, yet with it he sought to regulate all aspects of daily life: one's habits of mind, daily and weekly routines, and relationships with others. The monastery was a 'workshop' in which people learned to use these tools to shape a life together that was fulfilled.[1] Such a life was explicitly set apart from the social hierarchies and economic imperatives of the wider world, as one devoted to prayer and the 'care for souls'.[2] Although Benedict established core principles of humility, measure, common ownership, obedience, hospitality and stability, most of his rules were pragmatic rather than ideological: who should be served their dinner first, when to schedule lavatory breaks, etc. The *Rule* is preoccupied with all the gritty detail of everyday routines because these creaturely concerns are fundamental to the smooth running of a community – and if a community functions

Living meaningfully in time

Across these diverse practices, meaning takes shape as a verb rather than a noun, a doing rather than a thing. Abramović's endurance, Riley's rhythm, Wearing's photographs and Lemos's ritual propose different techniques for living in time. They also disclose inequalities of access, since the capacity to slow down or to contemplate depends on stability, care and space. A museum's stillness is not equally available to all. Yet, these works, even in their tensions, insist that meaning can be rehearsed anywhere through attention, patient return and acts of maintenance. The notion of eudaimonia – happiness as sustained virtuous activity – outlined by the Ancient Greek philosopher Aristotle, echoes through them.[17] To live meaningfully is not to chase joy but to practise it, moment by moment, until it becomes the texture of one's days.

We return to Mieke Bal, who warns that rigid periodisation in art history can obscure continuities.[18] Lives also resist neat segmentation. The so-called U-curve of happiness suggests that despair can turn again towards joy, that experience folds back on itself like Riley's chromatic rhythms, while Lemos's ritual garments braid memory with present urgency. Meaning arises in these folds where art, time and space meet. It gathers at thresholds and crossings. It appears in the pause that allows a colour to sing and in the breath that allows a word to land.

The quotation that opened this essay returns as a poetic suggestion rather than a verdict. To enter translucent and to depart multicoloured is to concede that time works upon us, tinting what was clear with the colours of encounter. The flourishing of life rests on an economy of gift and return: to give, to share and to receive within the river of days.

And if we seek an image, let it be Sisyphus on the slope. In the Greek myth, Sisyphus, a cunning king, offends the gods and is punished in the underworld. His sentence is to push a huge boulder up a hill; each time he nears the summit, the stone slips and thunders back down. In Homer's *Odyssey* (Book XI), Odysseus glimpses him in this endless labour. Centuries later, Albert Camus, in *The Myth of Sisyphus* (1942), reads the tale as a parable for human life: our tasks may feel repetitive and absurd, yet meaning can be made in how we meet them. Read the scene as a map: the mountain is time, the stone the day we shoulder, the ascent our labour. Condemned to repetition, he is also granted a discipline. With each push he learns the grain of the rock, the turn of the wind, the patience of breath; the hill answers differently every time. The descent is chosen, the return is his art, and in that turning back there is a freedom no sentence can annul.

If the phrase 'the meaning of life' is to keep its force, let it name not an answer but a way of living: questions tended with patience, a steady becoming enriched by relation and a faithful labour to honour beauty and joy, as they appear, and as they pass, while we shoulder the day once more and trace, with each renewed ascent, a brighter seam along the hill.

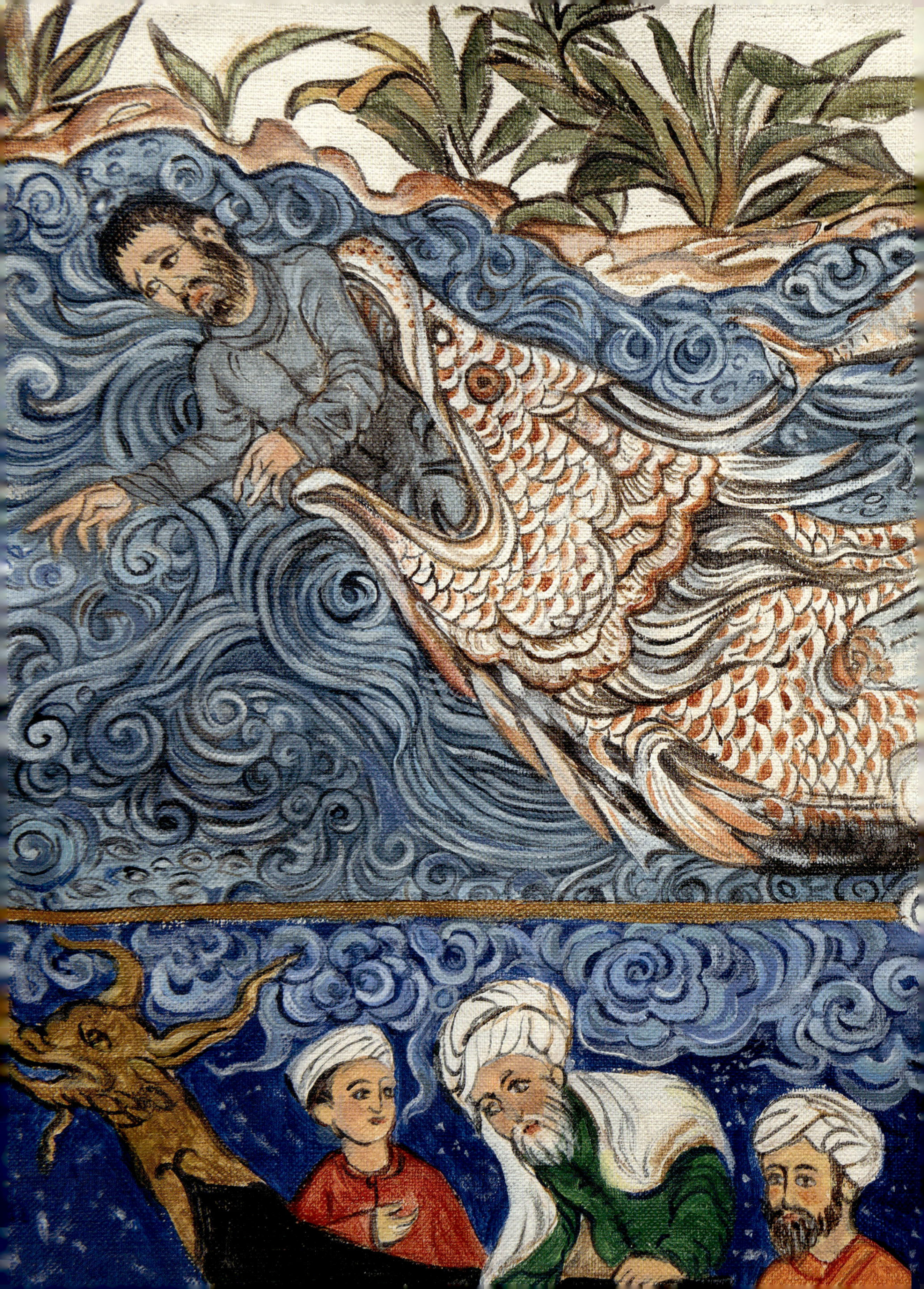

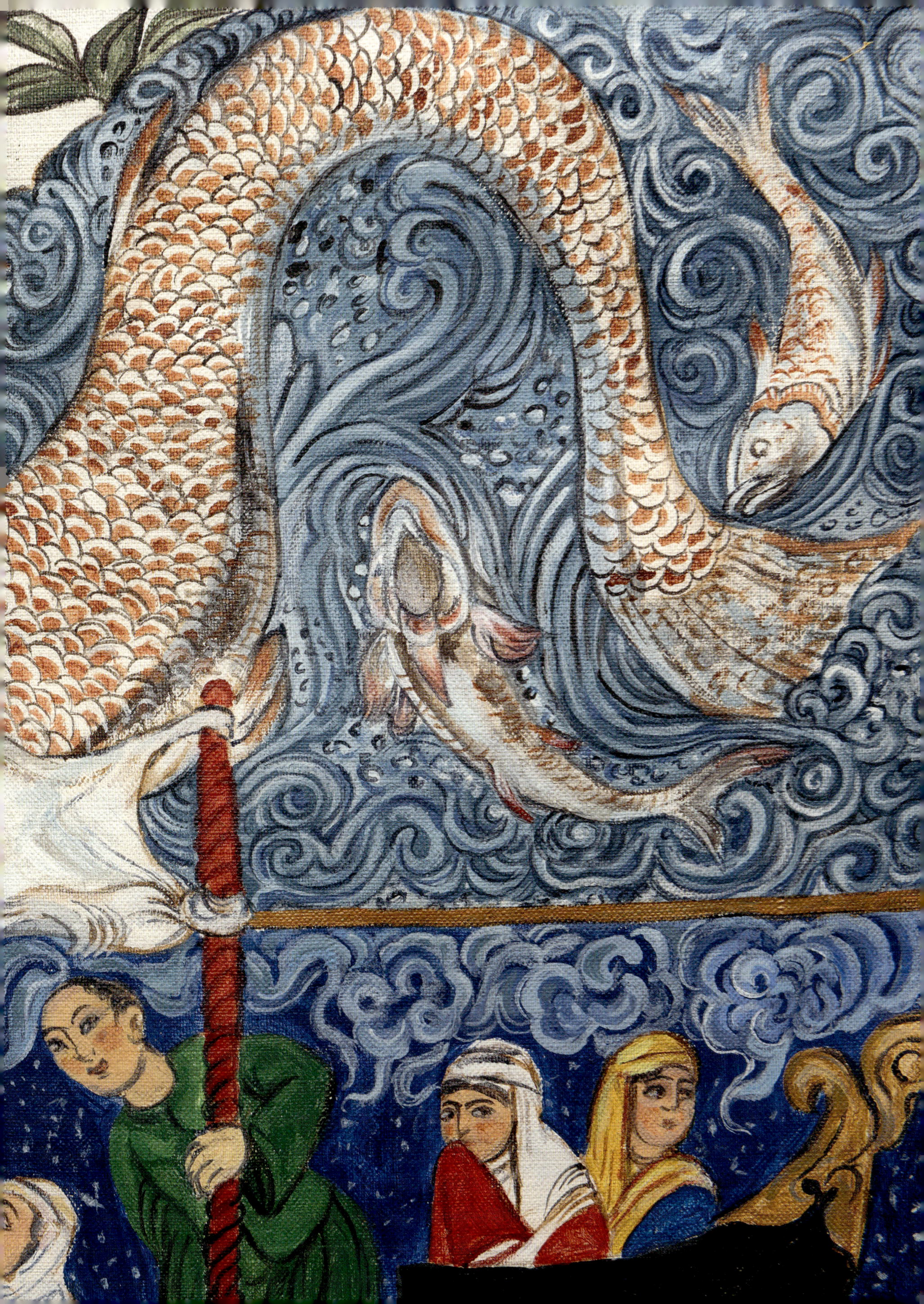

LIFE IN THE MULTIVERSE: LIBBY HEANEY

ROSY GRAY

In 2024, the Sainsbury Centre posed the question, 'What is the meaning of life?' to artist Libby Heaney (b.1983). In return, Heaney offered a deeply personal, generous and open account of the circumstances that led to the development of her work, *Life in the Multiverse* (2025), which explores this fundamental question.

Life in the Multiverse, a participatory digital installation using quantum computing, was conceived for the Sainsbury Centre's iconic Living Area as part of the *What is the Meaning of Life?* season. The Living Area has been home to the Sainsbury Centre's permanent collection since the museum opened in 1978, with artworks from across the globe and from different time periods displayed alongside each other. Deliberately disrupting traditional approaches to the classification of artworks in museums, the Living Area offers instead a window into making art as a universal and global phenomenon. As Heaney describes:

> What struck me most when visiting the Living Area were all the different gazes ... I felt like I was being stared at across space and time. The creators of these works made a quantum leap, transmitting to me in the here and now what it meant to them to be human through object form.[1]

For Heaney, *Life in the Multiverse* deliberately situates the season's question as subjective and individual, and, at the same time, universal and cosmic, inviting people to feel part of something bigger than themselves. Heaney does this by drawing on ideas around quantum forms of existence and, more specifically, the non-binary universe – or multiverse. In the multiverse, Heaney explains, a series of parallel worlds branch off from each other, and while each world is assumed to be separate and inaccessible to others, all worlds exist in the same physical space. For Heaney, the multiverse and, more broadly, the abstract qualities of quantum physics, were an unexpected form of comfort when her sister, Sally, died suddenly in 2019. Heaney describes her attempts to reconcile this devastating loss with her own belief systems, being forced to confront the nature of human existence.

> When Sally passed, I liked to imagine her still playing and laughing somewhere in the multiverse, inaccessible to me, yet predicted to exist. And I can still feel her love at the most unexpected moments.[2]

Life in the Multiverse builds on an existing body of work that explores both Heaney's intensely personal experiences of grief, and, more broadly, how the universal experience of loss is often accompanied by questions about the meaning of life. As Heaney explains, the questions that have underpinned her subsequent work are fundamentally around what happens when you die, what quantum physics can tell us about life and death and, in turn, the complexities of grief – how we, as humans, 'try to process things that are incomprehensible to us'.[3] Indeed, Heaney's

Sainsbury Centre Living
Area, 2025

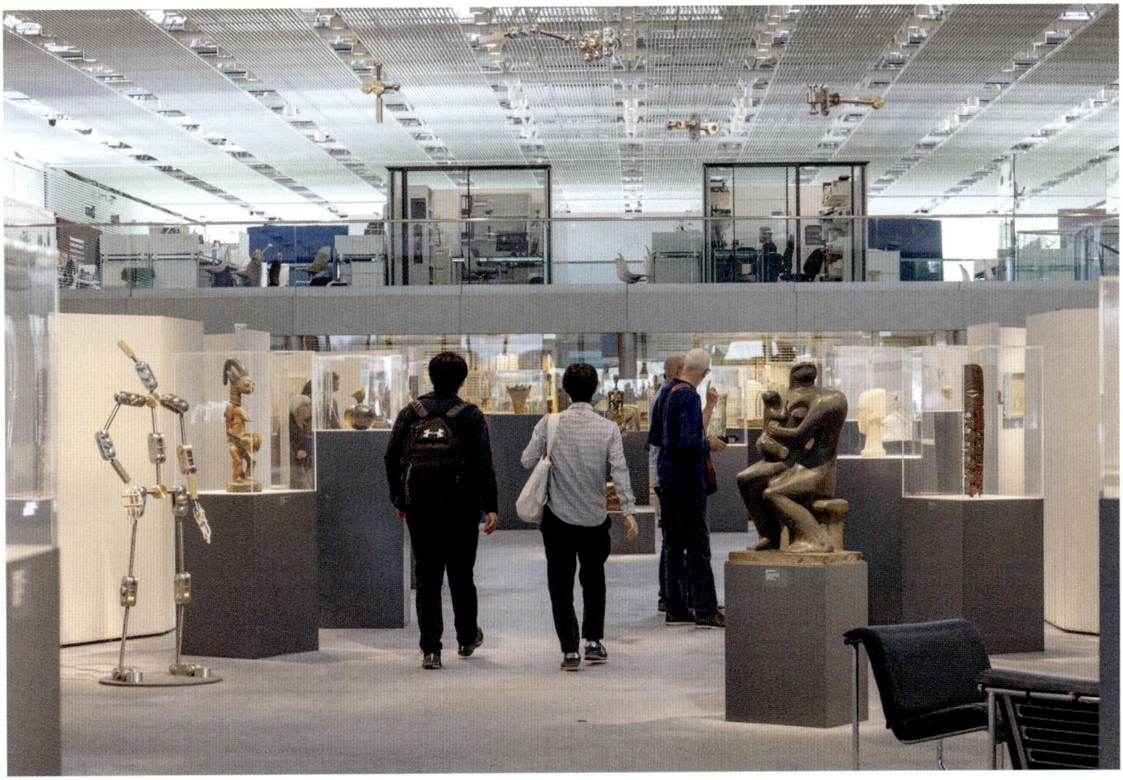

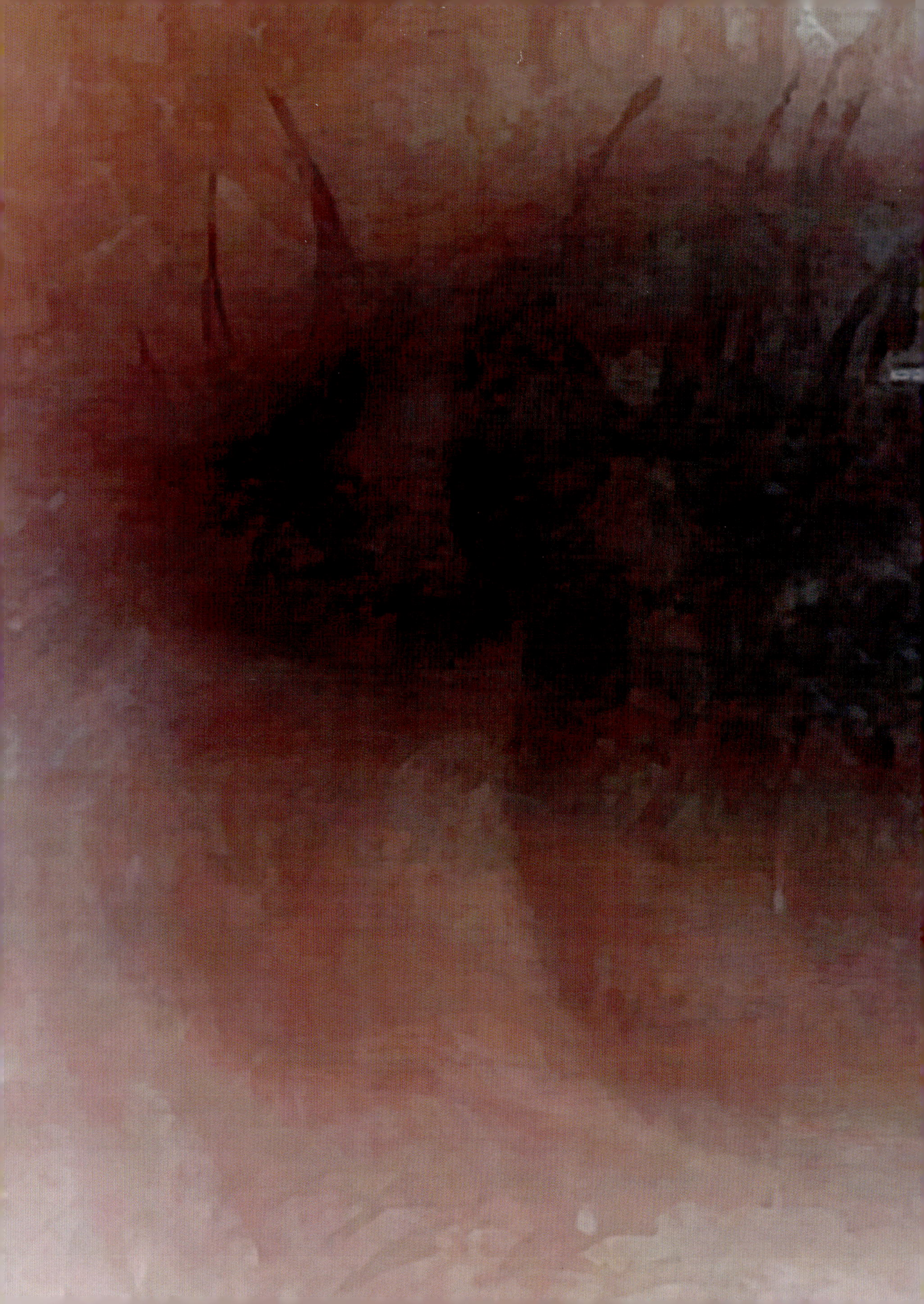

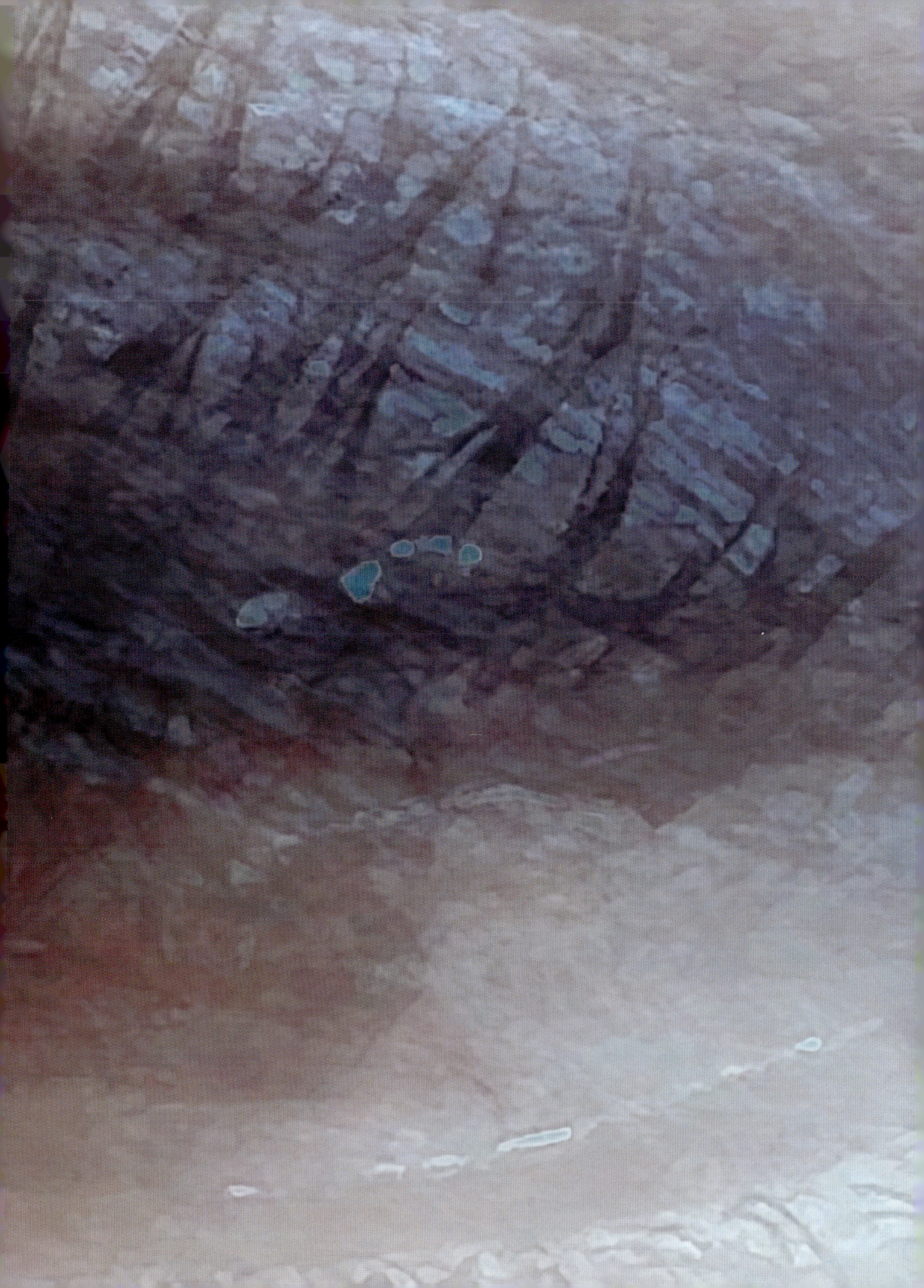

[previous page] Libby Heaney, *Never Too Much*, 2023, single-channel HD video, 18 mins. Private collection

highly immersive and interactive works encourage us to reflect on, and connect with, the different elements that make us human, both physically and emotionally. And perhaps unsurprisingly, it is the physical body that features so prominently in works such as *Please Don't Cry* (2023) and *Never Too Much* (2023), which focus on the eye and mouth respectively, with Heaney describing these physical features as being like portals into our inner worlds, 'liminal spaces of transformation'.[4]

Please Don't Cry, first exhibited as part of Heaney's solo show *Quantum Soup* at HEK Basel in 2024, is a single-channel video with no sound, in which we see an eye – the artist's own – crying while thinking about her sister's death. In the work, we are immersed in multiple, layered footage of the eye, created using quantum technologies. In 2019, the IBM quantum computer became publicly available via the cloud for the first time in the UK, and so Heaney started to experiment, writing code to create quantum entanglement. In effect, the data from this code creates a moving image, or rather a series of layered moving images, which, when played all at once, become more or less visible, depending on the relationship between the different entanglements. Or as Heaney describes it, how the different videos rise to the top and then decay.[5] The result, an exquisitely immersive ebb and flow of moving images washes in, around and over us.

This ambiguous shifting surface, in which the eye and tear are sometimes distinguishable but not entirely fixed, is mesmerising and disorientating in equal measure. As Heaney explains, one of the main concepts behind her work is the principle of quantum superposition, in which an entity – an atom or particle – can exist in more than one contradictory state at the same time. In *Please Don't Cry*, the eye sometimes takes on a vulvic form, which Heaney describes as emerging haphazardly throughout the work and alludes to 'the socio-historical conception of emotions and hysteria as a feminine weakness'.[6] In doing so, the work offers a riposte both to these broader narratives – a quantum, non-binary world in which feeling and logic can exist simultaneously – and to the artist's own personal narrative, in which her family express negative attitudes around showing overt displays of emotion.[7] At other points, the tear becomes more visible, sliding quickly over the surface of the eye and disappearing into the frame.

The flickering, blurry, dream-like movement of the eye is captured in what Heaney describes as 'quantum wave-like patterns'.[8] These 'wave-like' forms in turn point to collective, physical experiences of grief, metaphors that also reveal themselves in language. We talk, for example, about 'waves of grief' overwhelming us, often unexpectedly, in a way that feels much more aligned with physical experiences of grief within the body. Talking in a recent podcast for the Museum of Modern Art, New York, Cole Imperi explains how grief has historically been misunderstood as an emotion. As a thanatologist – a person who studies grief and death – Imperi explains that grief itself is not actually a feeling:

Libby Heaney, *Please Don't Cry*, 2023, single-channel video, 34 mins. Private collection

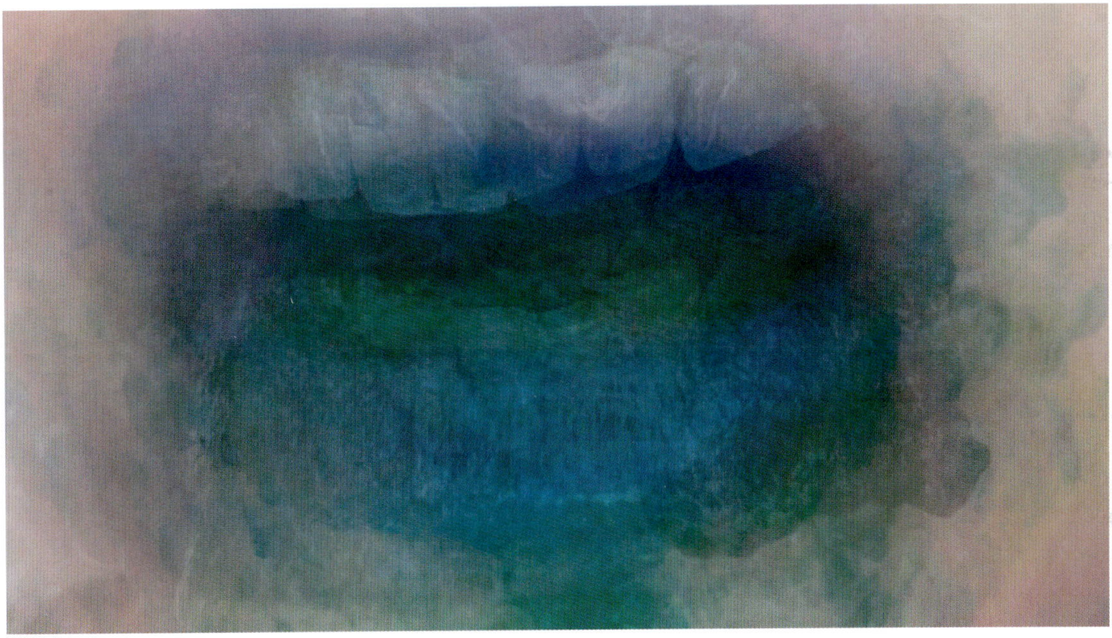

> You can feel sadness, anger, rage, despair, hopelessness. Those are all emotions, and those can be part of grief ... we now know that grief actually manifests in each person across six different categories. The six categories are: physical symptoms, emotional, spiritual, social, cognitive, and behavioural ... So when someone is grieving, it is a mind, body, spirit experience, truly.[9]

For Imperi, 'some of the most beautiful, captivating, emotive work [comes] from the moment when an artist is processing their own loss'.[10]

These embodied experiences reveal themselves across Heaney's broader practice. In *Never Too Much*, Heaney again employs her own body and quantum technologies to think about the impact of grief *within* the body, as much as its appearance outside. In this work, we encounter the artist's mouth, as she films herself swallowing, sucking, regurgitating and gagging on a slime-like substance. Slime is often used by Heaney, with the artist describing the possibilities inherent in its unstable nature. In *Never Too Much,* slime, like the metaphorical waves of grief, flows in and out of the body. As with *Please Don't Cry*, this footage is layered and interwoven, with the artist describing their 'opacity and transparency determined by the intricate relationships formed within the quantum realm'.[11] This layering, suggests Heaney, symbolises how emotion is held in the body 'as one experiences different feelings and sensations simultaneously. The result is a blurry, indeterminate aesthetic, which symbolises the self.'[12]

In *Heartbreak and Magic* (2024), Heaney develops this approach, combining quantum computing and virtual reality technologies for the first time in her work. Presented at Somerset House, London, and HEK Basel in 2024, the work places particular emphasis on the notion of telepresence – being present in another world or another space without physically existing there. As Heaney describes:

> Virtual reality felt like the best medium for the work because it really allows me to change reality in magical and unusual ways. For instance, some objects can morph and spread out in space and time, and the viewer can occupy a different body or experience things in ways that you couldn't in the physical world.[13]

For Heaney, this notion of embodiment is fundamental to how people experience *Heartbreak and Magic*. Combining virtual reality and multimedia drawings, the installation is an intuitive and embodied experience – an approach that extends to the physical environment in which the work is presented, as much as the work itself. The

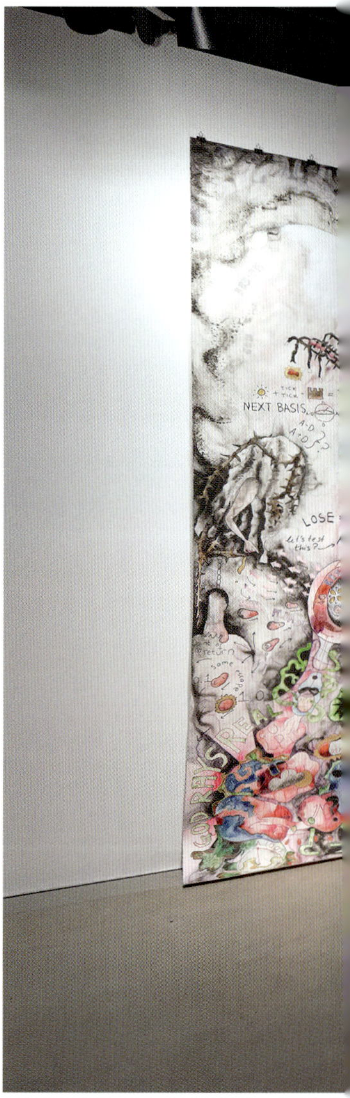

Libby Heaney, *Heartbreak and Magic,* 2024, installation view. HEK Basel

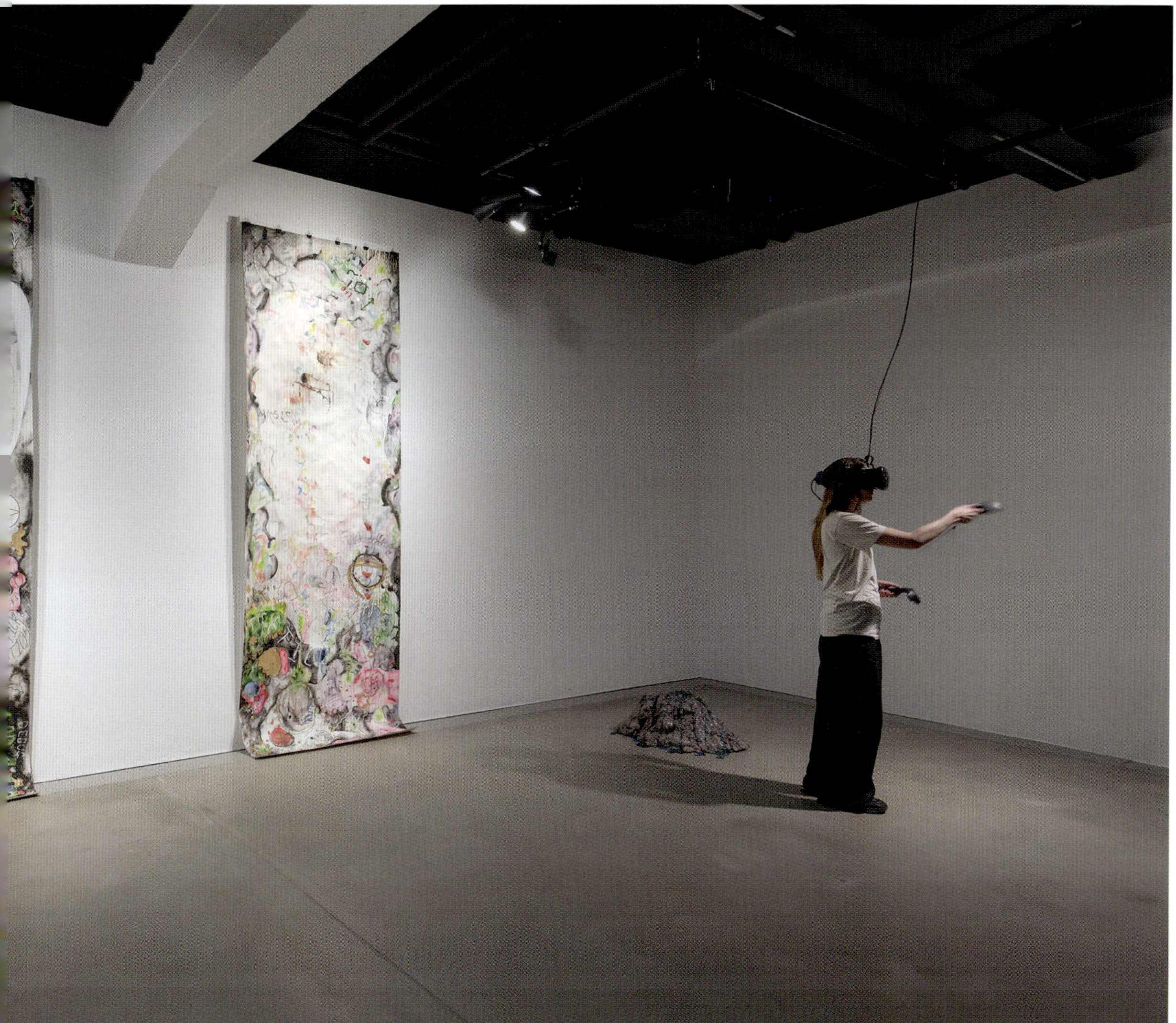

Libby Heaney, *Life in the Multiverse*, 2025, digital-quantum study

soft seating, curtains and furnishings invite people to enter a comforting, reflective space, in which pausing is actively encouraged. These feelings of comfort are extended across the installation, with scrolling, wave-like watercolours hanging from the walls. It is perhaps surprising to learn that when Heaney first started working with quantum computing in 2019, the initial step was, in fact, through watercolour. Heaney describes needing to start with an image so she could explore how the quantum effects would affect it visually. For Heaney, watercolour reminded her of working with a material like a quantum particle. She explains that while watercolour isn't a quantum particle, it feels magical and shares similarities, in the sense that it floods the page, spreads out and creates puddles that 'entangle' together.[14]

In Heaney's work, this notion of quantum entanglement articulates different feelings and sensations simultaneously, inviting us into dream-like, magical, cosmic and non-linear worlds. For Heaney, entangling provides a framework in which to consider, or reconsider, human and non-human connection and how we generate meaning. The self, when viewed through a quantum lens, is not an individual identity, but one interconnected with others - an emotional ecosystem. In moving away from the sequential logic of the digital binary computer, we're offered alternative positions in which our relationship with others is disrupted and transformed, as much as our sense of time and space. For Heaney, these principles open and invite very different conversations with artworks in the Sainsbury Centre's Living Area. Heaney entangles with them in embodied ways through practices such as meditation, capturing their gazes as she stares into their collective eyes, performing reiki and filming mutual points of connection, both physical and metaphorical. Heaney attempts to sonify the artworks, capturing their resonant frequency, engaging with them through proximity with her own body as a starting point to consider each connection. As Heaney describes, this approach bypasses established modes of knowledge and instead engages with the artwork's aura, reaching out beyond language.[15] In doing so, *Life in the Multiverse* invites us into Heaney's non-linear worlds, layering multiple narratives, both real and imagined, to explore our inherent interconnectedness.

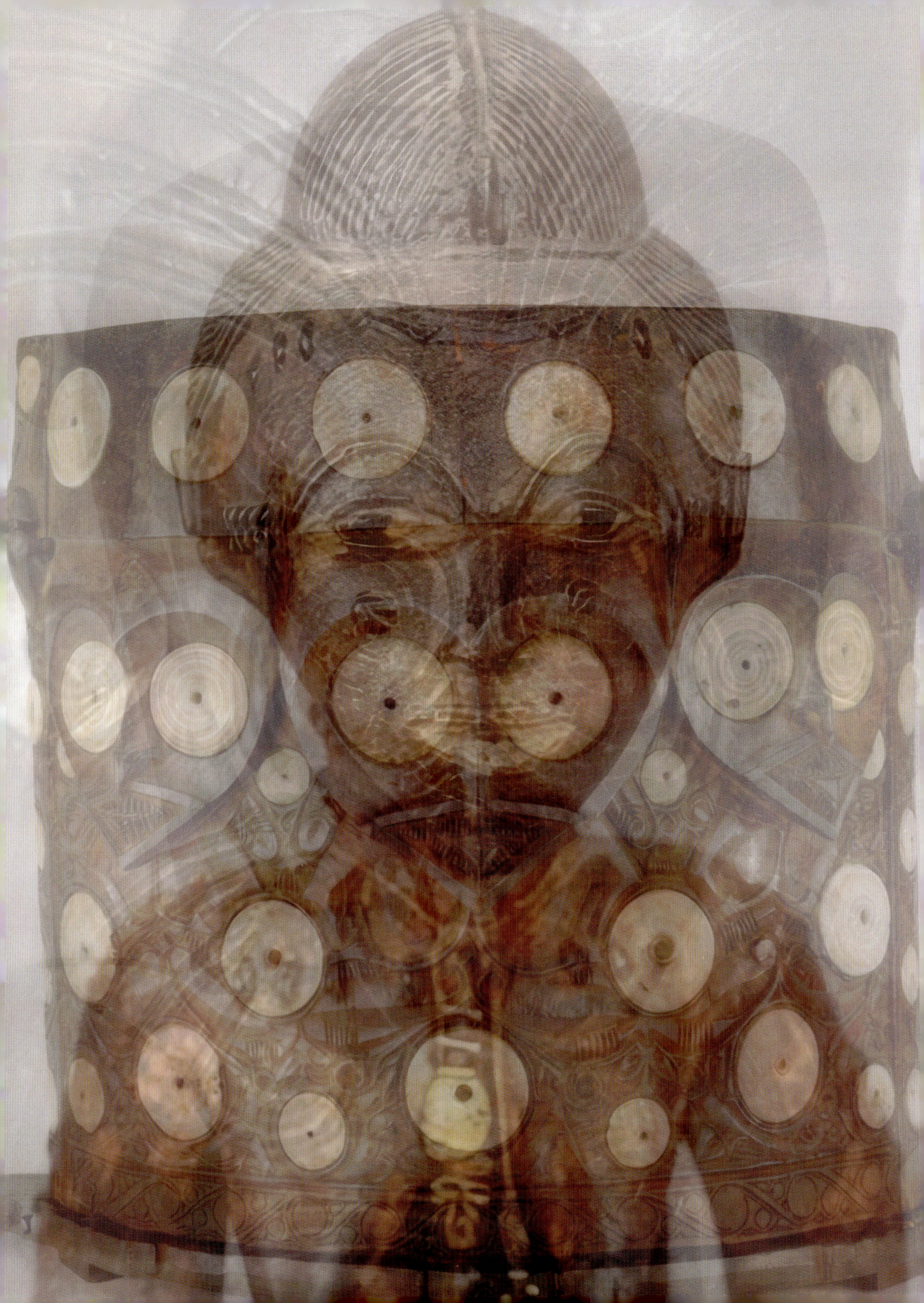

ACKNOWLEDGEMENTS

This publication accompanies the *What is the Meaning of Life?* season of exhibitions and projects running at the Sainsbury Centre from May to November 2026. We are incredibly grateful to the innumerable people whose generosity and knowledge have helped to create this series, only a fraction of whom we have space to name here.

The season was curated by an imaginative curatorial team to create a diverse and lively range of projects. The Sainsbury Centre's Head of Living Art, Rosy Gray, worked closely with Libby Heaney for *Life in the Multiverse*. Head of Exhibitions, Tania Moore, curated *Play Power*; Curator of Art and Climate Change, John Kenneth Paranada, curated *Joy Like Time*; and Learning Programme Manager (Adults and Young People), Nell Croose Myhill, developed a new strand of collaborative commissioning, working with artist Ruth Ewan to crowdsource plant stories and create a new artwork for *CATKINS FOREVER*. Rachel Anstey-Sanders, Learning Programme Manager (Children and Families), developed a 'Profound Play' project to be launched during the season; and Becca Sturgess, Learning Programme Manager (Schools and Outreach) and Lauren Wilson, Learning Programme Manager (Communities), developed new projects and partnerships for the season.

We were delighted to work with Dr Jessica Barker, Senior Lecturer in Medieval Art at The Courtauld, London, and Dr Ed Krčma, Associate Professor of Art History at the University of East Anglia, who brought their deep knowledge of, and innovative take on, medieval and contemporary art to curate *Living by the Rule: Contemporary Meets Medieval*. *Living by the Rule* has gathered many incredible and invaluable objects and artworks, including some of the earliest surviving medieval artefacts of their type. A number of these are exhibited together for the first time, or for the first time in decades. These complex loans would not have been possible without the generous support of a range of sponsors, including the Ruddock Foundation for the Arts, The Pilgrim Trust, Sam Fogg, Paul Mellon Centre, Idlewild Trust, The Leche Trust, Barbara Whatmore Charitable Trust, the International Centre for Medieval Art (ICMA), The Kress Foundation and the Worshipful Company of Clockmakers. We also thank the private sponsors and those who are not named for allowing all aspects of the exhibition to take place.

We would like to extend a sincere thanks to all those who have helped with the *Living by the Rule* exhibition. These include: Tuija Ainonen, Alexandra Ault, Pippa Balch, Nicolas Bell, Stacy Boldrick, Alixe Bovey, Claire Breay, Lindsay Macdonald Danckwerth, Michael Carter, Daniel Crouch, Timothy Davies, Lloyd de Beer, Simon Dell, Canon Peter Doll, Andrew Dunning, Stephen Eisenman, Ella Finney, James Freeman, Jana Gajdošová, Tamar Garb, Alanna Gedgaudas, Catherine Grant, Sarah Griffin, Ursula Griffith, Hannah Gruy, Roland Harris, Jack Hartnell, Sandy Heslop, Anna Himmelsbach, Fr. Stephen Horton OSB, Philippa Hoskin, Eleanor Jackson, Abbot President Christopher Jamison OSB, Joost Joustra, Rachel King, Susannah Kingwill, Laura Kuthan, Teresa Lane, Ariane Langreder,

Nicolas Linnert, Elizabeth McLean, Dale McFarland, Michael Newman, Tom Nickson, David Nowell-Smith, Kay Pallister, Matthew Reeves, Suzanne Reynolds, Vicki Rowlinson, Nicola Simpson, Jessica Smith, Naomi Speakman, Margit Thøfner, Gudrun Warren, Jonathan P. Watts, Cressida Williams and Michaela Zöschg.

Play Power is a cross-cultural and transhistorical exploration of how play is integrated (or not) throughout human societies, requiring a whole range of expertise. The exhibition's curator, Tania Moore, was delighted to be assisted by Samuele Tacconi while he was finishing his PhD at the University of East Anglia, with consultancy from Ben Highmore, Emeritus Professor of Cultural Studies at the University of Sussex and a Fellow of the British Academy. Other experts who informed the exhibition include Barbie Antonis and The Winnicott Trust; Thom Haley at Norwich University of the Arts; Dr Timothy Stott at the University of Dublin; Holly Tatham at Young V&A; Professor George Lau at the Sainsbury Research Unit; Dr Peter Moore at Audley End House and Gardens; Tom Wilson at the Design Museum; and colleagues at Infinite Form, especially Olivia Bone, Jason Elkins and Niky Ellison.

Joy Like Time has been made possible through the generosity, trust, and collaboration of the artists whose works shape the exhibition. We are deeply grateful to Marina Abramović, Gillian Wearing and Kalliopi Lemos for their openness, intellectual generosity, and the care with which they engaged in the development of the project. Their works and voices give form to the exhibition's central questions and have made this publication possible.

Our sincere thanks to the artists' galleries and studios for their invaluable support, guidance and professionalism throughout the lending, imaging and publication process. We are grateful to Ota Fine Arts and David Zwirner, and to Rachel Kent at Victoria Miro. We also extend our thanks to Lucy Price and Jonathon Cresswell at Maureen Paley, and to Arthur Yates, Phoebe Saatchi, Stefano Amoretti, Ying-Hsuan Tai, Raphael Del Bono and Carlotta Cerutti at Saatchi Yates. We are also grateful to Mark Sanders, Cathy Koutsavlis and Joe McMahon at the Marina Abramović Institute, to Paul Luckraft at Gazelli Art House, and to Rowan Durrant at Kalliopi Lemos's studio.

We thank all of the artists who have worked with us for the season. These include, but are not limited to: Marina Abramović, Seyi Adelekun, Pavel Büchler, Andrea Büttner, Peter Cook and his team, Moyra Davey, Tacita Dean, Rod Dickinson and Richard Barbrook, Ruth Ewan, Ryan Gander, Melanie Gilligan, Tom Hackney, Libby Heaney, Vincent James, Samuel Levi Jones, Vivienne Koorland, Joseph Kosuth, Kalliopi Lemos, Enzo Mari, Susan Morris, Eamon O'Kane, Yoko Ono, Olivia Plender, Bridget Riley, Leo Robinson, Kate Pickering, Ingrid Pollard, Elizabeth Price, Lucy Skaer, Christopher Stewart, Alison Turnbull, Gillian Wearing, Richard Wright, Danh Vo and Charlotte Zinsser. We thank all lenders who made the exhibitions possible with generous loans of incredible works of art from across the UK and beyond.

Dom Sylvester Houédard standing in his cream robes washing up at a sink, date unknown. Featured in the exhibition *Living by the Rule: Contemporary Meets Medieval*

The curatorial team expanded on the ideas within the season in illuminating new texts for this publication and we thank them all: Jessica Barker, Jago Cooper, Rosy Gray, Ben Highmore, Ed Krčma, Tania Moore, John Kenneth Paranada and Samuele Tacconi. The season was brainstormed by a group of artists, academics, life coaches and thinkers to help us conceive how to approach the theme. We are grateful to everyone who attended this creative think-in, generating a lively discussion, particularly the speakers Aribiah Attoe, Fiona Buckland and Libby Heaney.

The season's ideas were transformed into reality by a team of designers including Simon Leach and Symeon Banos at Simon Leach Design, who carried out the 3D exhibition design for *Living by the Rule* and *Play Power*, and David Sudlow Designers who conceived and executed the graphic identity for the season. George Sexton Associates executed the lighting design for the season and Paul Kuzemczak carried out the 3D design for *Joy Like Time*. This book was expertly designed by James Alexander at Jade Design and project managed by Lizzy Silverton. We thank everyone at Kulturalis, our publishing partner on the book.

We are grateful to our regular funders, including, but not limited to, the Gatsby Charitable Foundation and UKRI. John Kenneth Paranada's post is generously funded by the John Ellerman Foundation. Finally, these exhibitions and publications would not take place if it weren't for all the staff at the Sainsbury Centre who work incredibly hard to create and run these seasons for our visitors' enjoyment and enrichment, and we thank them all.

Idlewild Trust

The Leche Trust

Pilgrim Trust

RFA
THE RUDDOCK FOUNDATION FOR THE ARTS

SOCIETY OF ANTIQUARIES OF LONDON

SAM FOGG

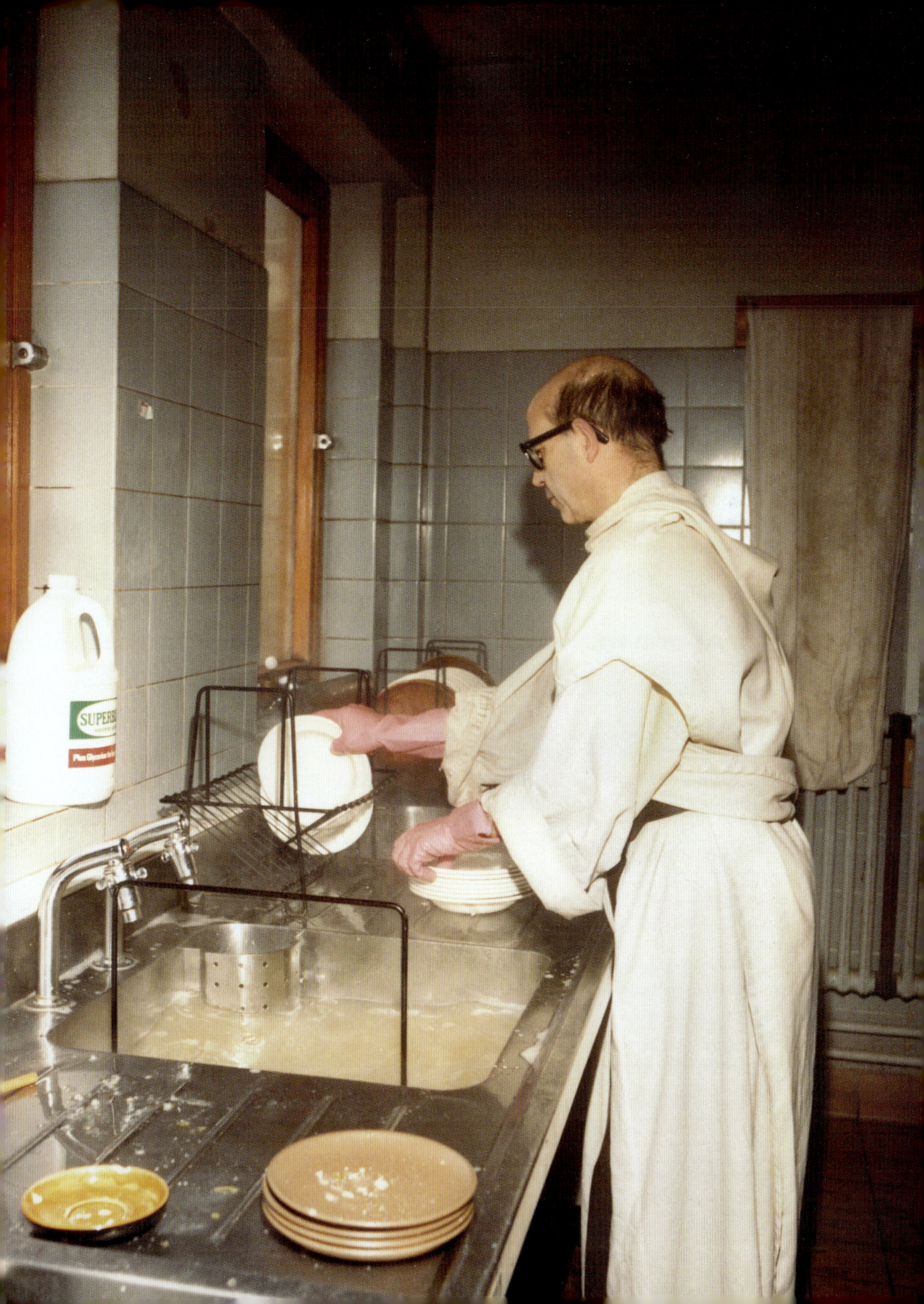

AUTHOR BIOGRAPHIES

Jessica Barker is Senior Lecturer in Medieval Art at The Courtauld in London. Her research focuses on sculpture from *c.*1200–1500 in northern Europe and Portugal, with a particular interest in questions relating to the body identity, and materiality. She has published widely, in journals including *Art Bulletin, Art History, British Art Studies, The Burlington Magazine, Gesta* and *The Sculpture Journal*. Her prize-winning book, *Stone Fidelity: Marriage and Emotion in Medieval Tomb Sculpture* (2020), explores the relationship between love and death in funerary art. She also sits on the Fabric Advisory Committee for Norwich Cathedral.

Jago Cooper is Executive Director of the Sainsbury Centre, and Professor of Art and Archaeology at the University of East Anglia. Jago has worked for and with museums, universities and heritage organisations around the world to explore and communicate aspects of the great human story. His books and publications provide innovative perspectives on cultural experience and interpretation of material expression. His research has ranged broadly across universal questions facing global society, including climate change, technological revolution and social innovation. Jago's recent publications include *Living Art Sharing Stories* (2023), *Mapping a New Museum* (2022), *Peru: A Journey in Time* (2021) and *Arctic: Culture and Climate* (2020).

Rosy Gray is Head of Living Art at the Sainsbury Centre. In her role, Rosy cares for over 5,000 artworks from across the globe, overseeing collections research, artist projects, conservation, loans and acquisitions. Joining the Sainsbury Centre in 2024, Rosy has previously developed collections, exhibitions and artist commissions across a range of public institutions in the UK. Her research interests focus on representations of the body in art and literature, with a particular emphasis on dress.

Ben Highmore is Emeritus Professor of Cultural Studies at the University of Sussex and a Fellow of the British Academy. Currently he is an Honorary Professor at the University of Liverpool attached to the Centre for Culture and Everyday Life. He is the author of 11 books, most recently *Lifestyle: How Taste Changed Class in Late 20th-Century Britain* (2023) and *Playgrounds: The Experimental Years* (2024). He is currently working on two book projects: the first is a monographic study of the abstract painter Sir Frank Bowling and the second is an exploration of the experimental nature of the humanities at a time of multiple, competing emergencies.